MW01659707

This book is a gift to:

Jack + Jo

From:

Debbie

On:

Christmas 2012

The Beauty of Spring

"A heartwarming, inspirational autobiography"

by

Debbie Schmid

Dear Jack + Jo,
It is such a blessing to have you back in the neighborhood. I am so thankful that God brought you into my life. May God bless you richly with His everlasting "Beauty of Spring."

In Christian Love,
♡ Debbie
2012
Prov 3:5-6

The Beauty of Spring

"A heartwarming, inspirational, autobiography"

by

Debbie Schmid

JOY PUBLISHING
P.O. Box 827
San Juan Capistrano, CA 92675

IBSN 0-939513-48-X

Printed in the United States of America.

JOY PUBLISHING
P.O. Box 827
San Jaun Capistrano, CA 92675

Dedication

In appreciation for life and for all the blessings I have been granted, I dedicate my book to God, my heavenly Father; his Son Jesus, my precious Lord and Savior; and to the Holy Spirit who dwells within me.

Dear Heavenly Father,
Let me be a sunbeam in
A dark and dying world.
In Jesus' name I pray,
Amen.

TABLE OF CONTENTS

Introduction

The Midwest was my home. I was born and raised in Illinois - later moving next door to Iowa. I always felt close to nature and I treasured the different seasons.

Summer was full of sunshine and adventure. Occasionally, the sky became cloudy and frightfully dark. Thunder boomed and shook the world around us. Sharp, gusty winds blew as the rain poured from the heavens above. But, before long, everything quieted down and we heard the birds singing while the rain water trickled by. Sometimes we enjoyed a beautiful rainbow as the clouds parted and the sun shone through.

Autumn was full of busy-ness. Children returned to school, farmers brought in their harvest and everyone prepared for the long, cold winter ahead. While coolness filled the air around us, our heavenly Father busily painted the landscape in beautiful shades of yellow, orange, and red.

When winter came, it dragged on and on. The gray skies and dreary days were depressing. The only beauty I found came from the purity and sparkle of the newly-fallen snow.

Spring was the highlight of the year! New life appeared in every direction. Trees and flowers budded. Before long, the landscape was fragrant and full of beautiful flowers. Our little feathered friends returned from the South bringing sweet music as they joyfully prepared new homes. The spring rains gently fell and the grass became green and alive again. Happiness and joy filled our hearts while the miracle of new life surrounded us.

As I recently searched through seventeen years of my personal journals, I uncovered a multitude of memories. Some were happy like summertime, giving me the warm feeling of sunshine and joy. Other memories were scary like thunderstorms, and still others were cold like winter, filling me with darkness and sorrow. Reading through them, I realized how much our lives are similar to seasons of a year.

We all face many trials during our lifetime. These trials mold and shape us. Some trials, however, bring dreariness into our lives that we refuse to release. Hanging on to those winters of darkness and depression binds us to a lifetime of unhappiness. Unless we allow the gentle whisper of God's Spirit to blow those dark clouds away, the sun won't shine and spring can't take its place.

I am a simple person, but I chose to write this book and share my life with you because my heart is filled with love and compassion for others. I pray that as you read, you can relate some of the situations to your own life and gain a new perspective on "The Beauty of Spring."

I

Two Little Girls

Heart defect! The words exploded over and over in the young mother's mind as she sat, stunned, staring at the doctor. She had brought six-week-old Debbie in for a routine check-up, and now she tried to grasp the importance of these two dreaded words. Heart defect!

How was this possible? She looked at Debbie kicking on the examining table. How could such a beautiful child hide such a terrifying secret? Surely the doctor was mistaken! He must be!

Debbie's mother struggled to listen as the doctor continued, "I want you to take her to Children's Memorial Hospital in Chicago. The specialists there can run tests to confirm my diagnosis and to determine the extent of the damage. It may take several weeks to get her in, so . . ."

The young mother left the doctor's office in shock. She clung to little Debbie, remembering the stormy December day a few weeks earlier when Debbie entered the world--and their hearts. The chill of that winter day was nothing compared to the chill that now gripped her.

Three months later, the seemingly endless wait was over. Debbie, now four months old, was seen at Children's Memorial Hospital (C.M.H.). The diagnosis was confirmed. Debbie's heart was defective, but it was still too early to predict how this would affect the little girl's life. The specialists advised her parents to treat her like a normal, healthy child. As nearly as they could tell, the problem was relatively minor and corrective heart surgery might be possible at a later date. Debbie's parents grasped at that hope. All they could do was to wait and hope.

As time passed, Debbie's motor skills and intelligence developed at a normal rate. She sat up, crawled, played, and walked like other babies. One of her favorite activities was playing in her food. Squashing it through her fingers and then smearing it on everything within reach was especially fun. Debbie's size, however, was a concern to the doctor. At the end of a year, she was very tiny and pale.

One day when Debbie was three years old, her nose began to bleed. After the usual first-aid measures did not stop the flow, her parents rushed her to the family physician who gave her an injection and packed her nose. Although the bleeding stopped, Debbie's breath suddenly became short and she turned blue. She was rushed to C.M.H. to combat her toxic reaction to the injection. It was three days before her condition stabilized enough for her to go home. Nosebleeds became a regular part of Debbie's life. Her mother spent hours lying awake at night, listening to Debbie breathe. Very early one morning, she was wakened by tiny sobs. She ran to Debbie's room and was shocked to find her daughter and all of the bedding saturated with blood. The young mother cautiously carried Debbie to the kitchen where she blotted her face with a warm cloth to remove the dried blood. Once again, she could not stop the flow of blood and emergency treatment was necessary.

Sometimes Debbie's blood loss was so great that she collapsed and had to be resuscitated. Her fingernails always had a bluish cast from lack of oxygen in her bloodstream, and her chest became deformed.

The time came for the heart specialists to determine the exact nature of Debbie's heart problem. When she was four years old, they decided to perform a heart catheterization. The procedure, while never pleasant, was more difficult than anticipated. In spite of the problems, however, the doctors were able to gain valuable information. The doctors originally suspected that there was a small hole in the wall between the heart chambers. Their main objective for the catheterization was to, specifically locate the defect and, make plans to correct it. Instead, they discovered the wall between the chambers was absent, thus making it impossible to correct. Since both oxygenated and unoxygenated blood mixed together within the heart cavity, this created high blood pressure in her lungs and caused even more complications. Heart surgery would be more risky than beneficial, so the doctors decided it was no longer an option at this time. All they could do was wait some more, and keep hoping.

Two weeks later Debbie was back in the hospital, having lost her appetite and all interest in her surroundings. She improved enough to go home, but was often rushed back by ambulance. Frequently she suffered spells in which her heart rate decreased and breathing became difficult. When her body fell limp from lack of oxygen, intravenous medicine was administered to give her heart the boost it needed to keep going. Her frail body became weaker as she struggled for life.

During her frequent hospital stays, her parents became acquainted with other parents whose children were hospitalized. Among them were the parents of a six-year-old girl named Carol. Carol's kidney disease was also critical and unstable, and sometimes the two girls shared the same room. Their mothers quickly became friends, comforting and supporting each other through the long, wearisome hours of sitting by their daughters' bedsides. Many times, after eating lunch together, they stopped by the hospital gift shop to select a toy or book for the little girls. It brought joy to the mothers to see their daughters' faces light up. What more could a mother do but be near her little one in time of need?

During one hospital visit when Debbie was four years old and Carol was seven, both mothers paced nervously in front of the Intensive Care Unit on the third floor. As they passed the windows, they struggled to catch glimpses of the girls. They needed reassurance that their daughters were still alive. Time seemed to stand still for the worried parents. Debbie's mother kept her hands and mind busy by knitting something beautiful. Carol's mother, however, prayed constantly for God's will to be done in the little girls' lives. On August 16, at Passavant Memorial Hospital, a few weeks after her two kidneys were transplanted, Carol's long and difficult struggle for life ended. Debbie continued to fight.

That fall when the school board met, they considered whether Debbie should be permitted to start school. She was not yet five, but, because of her poor health, the board decided it might be good for her to get an early start. That way, if she missed a lot of school and had to be retained, she would still not be older than her classmates. Debbie was bright enough to keep up academically, even though she was socially immature.

Debbie's condition worsened as time passed, and that December when she was almost five years old, the doctors told her parents there was little hope for their daughter. Debbie weighed only twenty-seven pounds and frequently suffered with severe migraine headaches which medicine was unable to relieve. Everyone, including the school bus driver, carried her in their arms because she was physically unable to walk. Debbie never complained, however, she became a very frightened child. Time was short.

One bitterly cold day in January, just one month after her fifth birthday, Debbie was struck with another severe attack. Her father hurried to the garage for the oxygen tank as her mother summoned an ambulance. Debbie grasped at her father's arms, fighting for each breath. Her eyes dilated and her chest ached with pain as her heart rate continued to fall. Suddenly she collapsed in her daddy's arms. The ambulance rushed her to Children's Memorial Hospital emergency room. As Debbie's parents paced anxiously, they remembered other times when Debbie had fought for life. Each time she had beaten the odds. Could she do it one more time?

Once again Debbie pulled through. Unlike Carol's parents, Debbie's parents were given the chance to raise their little girl. It was, indeed, a miracle from God.

I am Debbie--that little girl who was blessed with the gift of life. As I continue to share my life story with you, I hope you will understand just how precious life is. Though not always easy, life is good.

I asked a doctor one time what keeps me going. This was her reply: "Somehow when you were in the womb, nature tipped your heart and it rests in a very unusual position. That is why you do so well." How sad that she gave credit to "nature." I praise God,

"For you created my inmost being; you knit me together

in my mother's womb. I praise you because I am fearfully and wonderfully made; Your works are wonderful, I know that full well" (Psalm 139:13-14).

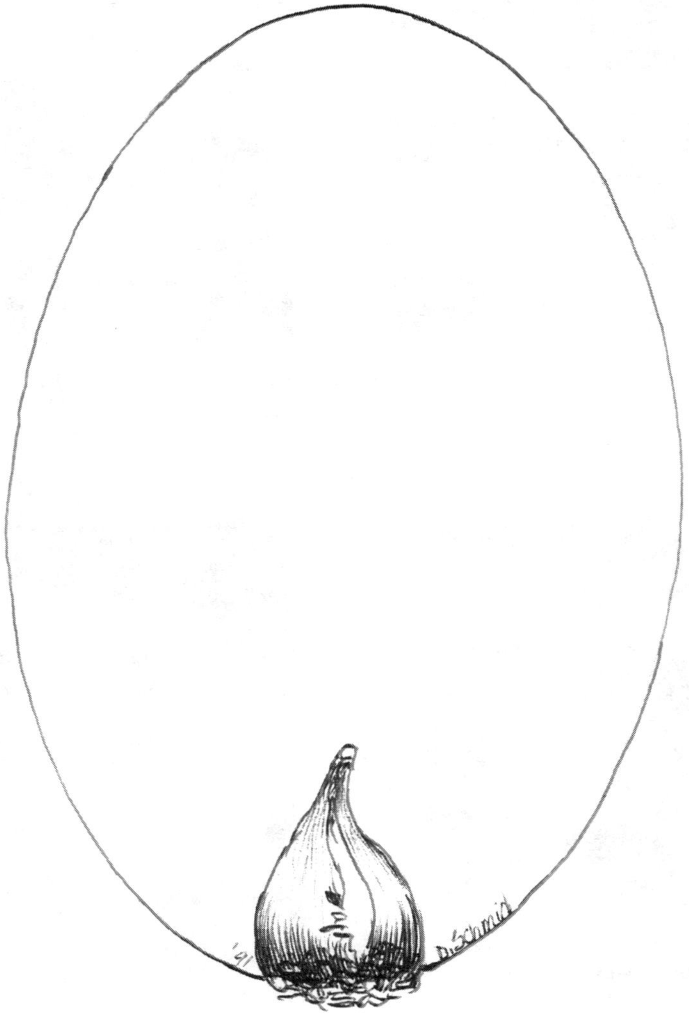

A Little Girl with a Terrifying Secret!

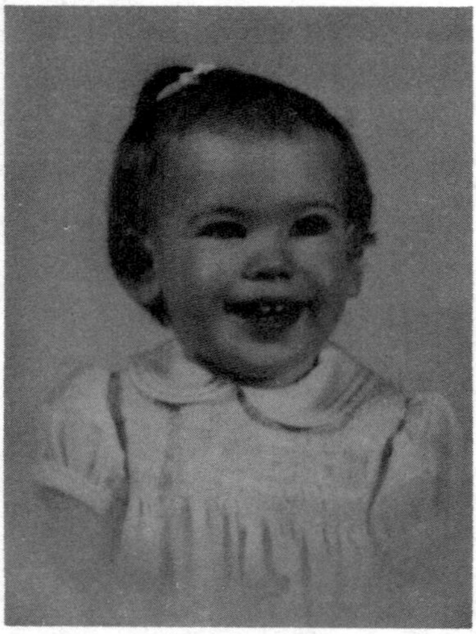

1 year old

Summertime fun
1½ years old

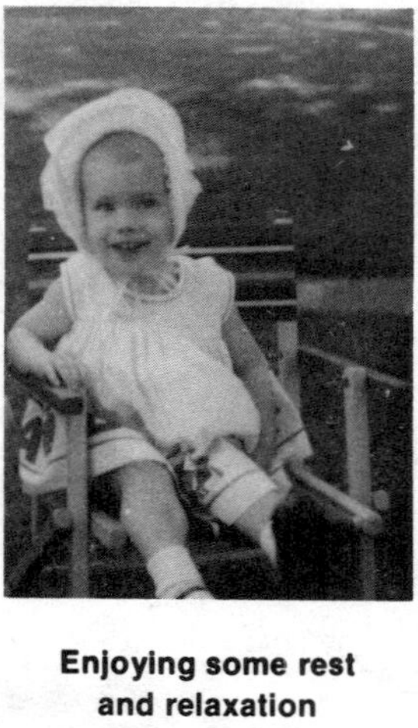

Enjoying some rest
and relaxation
1½ years old

Christmas morning
4 years old

II

One Unhappy Family

Mom hung up the phone, slammed her hand down on the counter, and muttered through clenched teeth, "He's lying. I hate it when your uncle lies to me!"

The table was set and smells of supper hung in the air. The eyes of four hungry children were turned toward her. "Same old story. Your uncle says your father just left. We'll give him half an hour. Now," she turned to us, "all of you scoot out of the kitchen. Go play a little longer."

We all knew what came next, even my youngest brother who was just a toddler. We knew Dad's truck was still parked at his brother's tavern, ten minutes' drive away. Half an hour and another phone call later, we all piled into the car and headed down to what I call the "Broken Family Saloon." As we pulled into the parking lot, we could see Dad's truck.

"It's Debbie's turn to go in this time," volunteered my younger brother, three years younger than me. "I went in last time."

"Can't someone else go?" I begged. I hoped my older brother would be drafted for the job. "I don't want to."

"Run in and get your father, Debbie." Mom was firm. I dreaded going down the steps toward the dark, smoke-filled room. As I opened the door, I was nearly knocked backward by a wave of loud music and the sickening smell of alcohol. I fought to keep from vomiting. I stood shaking as I looked down the row of drunks, trying to pick out the one who was my daddy. I walked slowly over and put my hand on his arm. "Daddy, come home now." I begged.

"Okay," he mumbled. "Okay. Just one more. Then I'll come home."

"Come now."

"Just one more."

Back I trudged up those stairs, gulping in the fresh air, knowing full well that he would not come. Not even after "one more." Then came the silent drive home and the over-cooked supper. We all knew we could look forward to a fight when Dad finally got in that night, whatever time that might be. Many times my brothers and I huddled together in the darkness listening to Dad and Mom argue. I often hid under a bed or in a closet listening to the sounds of yelling, slamming doors, and profanity echo through our neatly-kept house. I always wondered if the sheriff would be necessary again. Life was so unpredictable and frightening.

Sometimes, when the fighting was especially bitter, Mom and Dad called us out of hiding, stood us between them, and demanded that we tell them whose fault it was that our family was in this mess. What could we say? If we singled out either parent, the other was furious. It didn't take long to learn the safest answers were either, "You're both wrong," or, "I'm not getting involved."

I often left little notes in Dad's truck, lunch box, or shirt pocket, begging him to stop drinking. I explained that I loved him, but that his drinking was hurting our family. Those little letters never seemed to make any impression on him. As a result, I felt rejected and unloved.

The evenings when Dad came straight home were wonderful. His warm smile, understanding spirit, and sense of humor made him a delight to be around--when he was sober. On cold winter days, when it was impossible for him to lay brick, I remember him in the kitchen making homemade chicken-noodle soup and cinnamon rolls for our dinner. What a treat! But, as I grew up, those sober times became fewer and farther apart.

Dad took a very relaxed approach to raising kids. His advice to us was, "Do whatever you want to, have fun doing it, but, for heaven's sake, don't get caught!" Mom, on the other hand, gave us the discipline and stability we needed to face life. She was the backbone of the family. She was the one who prepared delicious hot meals day in and day out, holding them until all hours for Dad. She was the one who sewed beautiful clothes, not only for me, but also for my dolls. She was the one who saw that our clothes were clean and pressed and that our socks matched the rest of our outfits. In later years she was the one who made sure I always left home wearing something modest and didn't have my face plastered with make-up. She was the one who insisted on respect and demanded to know where we were going, with whom, and when we would return. But, as Dad's drinking continued and her unhappiness deepened, she often withdrew into a bitter silence that was difficult for us to understand. When her temper flared and she was sharp with us, we did not understand that it was Dad and her situation that upset her, and not us.

I always longed for some kind of encouragement and praise from my parents, but it just was not there. There were so many times when I really needed a hug or to hear them say, "You're a good daughter," or "I love you." Dad did sometimes, but usually when he was drunk and that didn't count.

In bed at night, I tried to sort out my family's problems. I didn't understand why suddenly my daddy's drinking became an addiction. He had always been so gentle and caring, especially when I was ill. That was it! He drank because I was sick! Over and over I came to the conclusion that the problems were my fault. If I weren't so sickly, I thought, there wouldn't be so many bills and Dad wouldn't have to work so many jobs. He wouldn't be under so much stress and maybe he wouldn't drink. And if he didn't drink, there wouldn't be the fights and maybe Mom wouldn't be so angry all the time. I thought it was my fault that my parents were unhappy. It was a frightening burden for a little girl to bear. As I lay in the darkness, I clutched my stuffed bunny and cried myself to sleep.

First Grade
A quick photo
without a face mask on

A "little" Brownie Girl Scout
8 years old

Trying to fit in at Girl Scout Camp
12 years old

Receiving my first Class Badge
as a Cadette Girl Scout
13 years old

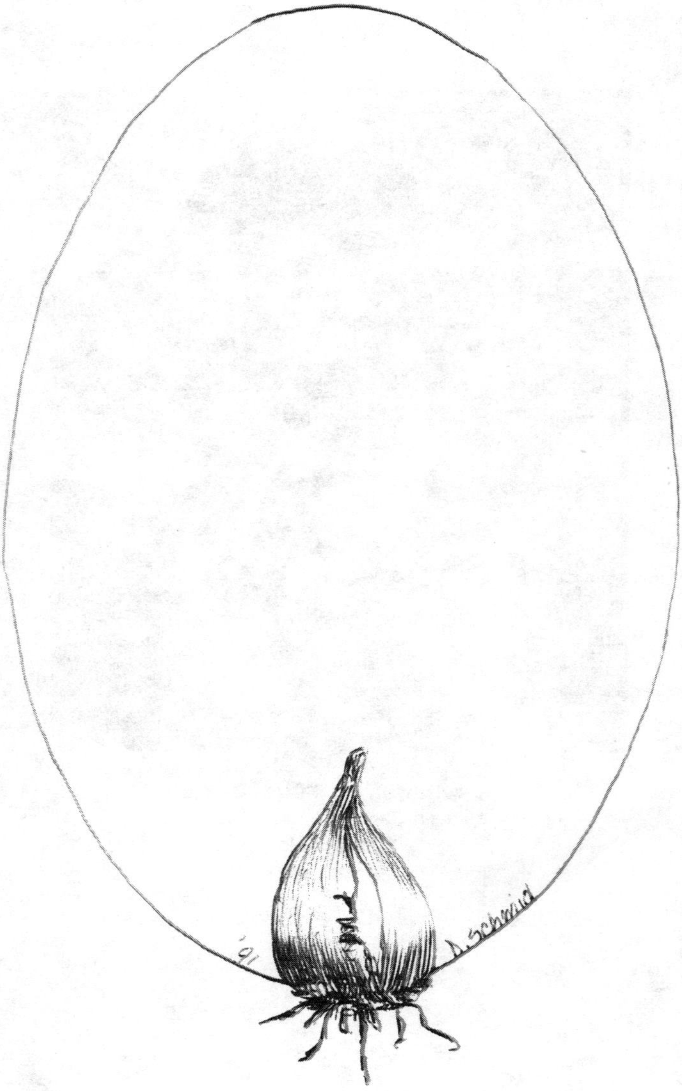

III

From "Skinny Bones" to "Flatsy"

I tried to remain calm as I turned the dial on the combination lock one more time. "Take it easy, Debbie," I kept telling myself. It didn't help having my girlfriend jiggling the door from the inside.

"Kim, just a minute!" I pleaded. "Stop banging."

"Are you getting it?" came her muffled cry.

"I'm trying. The lock is stuck." I fought to hold down panic. What had started out as a funny joke was suddenly not so funny anymore. What was I to do? My best friend was trapped in her school locker and it was my fault! I wondered if she would still be my friend after she got out.

"Kim, I'm going to get help," I hollered through the metal door.

"Hurry!"

I ran down the hall looking for a grown-up. Where were they when you needed one? I sped toward the teachers' lounge. At last! The relief of having my friend out was definitely worth the embarrassment of having to tell a room full of teachers what I had done.

Kim and I had been friends since the spring of fourth grade. Up until then, I didn't really have any friends in school. None, except the school nurse.

For the first three years or so of school, it must have been rather frightening to have me in class--for the teacher and the students. Sometimes I was so weak I was unable to walk down the hall and had to be pushed in a chair. Mrs. Bridges, the school nurse, sat with me during many lunch hours trying to coax me to eat. On bad days, my teacher sent for Mrs. Bridges. She often found me with my head down on my desk and my entire body blue from lack of oxygen. More than once the nurse drove me home to my mother's care. One time in particular, I was barely responding. Mrs. Bridges was very frightened for me, but my mom always appeared calm and knew exactly what to do.

Despite the fact that my health situation continued to stabilize as I grew older, I always had extra burdens to bear. In winter I stayed indoors during recess because I could not tolerate the cold. I watched the children running and playing outside and sometimes peering in the windows.

"Hey, Privileged!" they yelled through the glass. Sitting alone in the classroom without friends and not being able to run and play was not my idea of being privileged. When I did have to go outside, either coming to school or leaving, I bundled up in layers of sweaters, coats, scarves, and, worst of all, a face mask. The other children found the mask so funny. "Why do you wear half of your mother's bra on your face?" they laughed. Although Mom always kept me neatly dressed in feminine dresses, I didn't look quite like other kids. I acquired nicknames like "Purple Lips," "Pale Face," and "Skinny Bones." How those names stung! I was ashamed of the way I looked. Why did I have to be so small and ugly? So many times I turned my face to hide the tears and swallowed the lump in my throat. I tried not to show the hurt, because if I broke down and cried, then I was "Big Baby."

Although school work did not present much problem, making friends did--at least until my fourth grade teacher insisted that Kim and I become friends. She didn't actually make us be friends, but she insisted that we play together--to the embarrassment of both of us. However, as we began to play and talk to each other, we discovered we had a lot in common, and we became very close.

I often became discouraged because I could not participate in strenuous physical recreation, but my frustrations faded when I became active in scouting and spent several summers at scout camp. Cooking over an open fire, singing new songs (even though I can't carry a tune in a bag), making crafts, slapping mosquitoes, and sharing secrets made fun and exciting times.

One thing I was never able to conquer was passing the beginners' swimming test, even after six years of trying. Therefore, I was not allowed to go on canoe trips. I was also unable to ride along with the others on bicycle outings. These situations made me feel defeated, however, Louie, the camp caretaker, chauffeured me to destinations in the camp pick-up truck so I wouldn't miss all the fun. This helped me to feel better emotionally because I felt like I fit in "somewhere". On hikes, the counselor always insisted on bringing along "Junior" (a little red wagon which I, or others with health problems, rode in, if necessary). I found it embarrassing when friends fussed about who would pull me in Junior. How I wished I could hike like everyone else!

I always enjoyed earning badges and was so proud to have Mom sew each new one on the sash of my uniform. In my last year of Junior Scouting, the leader gave up the troop. I had many limitations as to what I could do, and because I enjoyed scouts so much, Mom decided to take over. That way I could complete that section of scouting. After I advanced to Cadettes, Mom kept the troop for several more years.

Though grade school was sometimes difficult, junior high was worse--especially gym class. I still could not participate in the actual class, but the teacher required me to dress down, watch, and write a report on the sport. I was also required to shower after each class. I still wore a little girl's size 6x and, since I was a late bloomer, the bump on my chest, caused by my heart condition, was very obvious. I soon became known as "Flatsy" or "Lumpy Chest." I learned quickly to fudge my way through the shower room without removing my underclothing. I just lowered my T-shirt straps (I didn't even need a bra!) and wrapped the towel around the middle section of my body. Then, running through the showers, I wet only my legs, arms and face. As I passed the teacher, I called out my number, appearing clean and showered! After that, I rushed into a bathroom stall to dress in private. It worked beautifully until someone snitched on me. I tried to explain to the teacher, but she insisted that I shower correctly. I refused. I had put up with the embarrassment of showering as long as I could. I took a demerit every day instead. That gave me a D- on my report card, but I didn't care. To me, it was worth it.

No more was I willing to just "take it" when humiliated. One day in P.E. class one of the girls made me so angry I started a fist fight with her. Never mind that she was almost twice my size. I didn't receive a scratch, but she took a beating! We were promptly ordered upstairs to the principal's office where he insisted that I apologize to her. I refused! He threatened to suspend me for misconduct. That didn't bother me, either. Then at least no one could tease me. However, I hated to think how disappointed my mom and dad would be if I went that far. The principal gave me one minute to make my choice. I watched the second hand go around the clock for fifty-nine seconds, then blurted out, "Sorry, but I'm really not!" He dismissed us. Later that girl and I became friends and even stood up in each other's weddings. Years later, we often laughed about that fight. She always said afterwards, "I never knew such a skinny little kid could be so strong!"

Another time, a boy in my math class called me "Purple Lips" loud enough so everyone in the class could hear him and laugh. I calmly walked up to his desk and overturned it--with him sitting in it! His books flew everywhere. Then I quietly went back to my own desk and sat down. The whole class stared at me in shock. I was surprised myself.

My very first date was exciting. A movie, pizza, and a good-night kiss. My older brother saw us at the movie and teased me about it for weeks afterwards. Passing notes in the hall, winking and joking with my date, went on for weeks. Then I was invited to a party. Wow! Was I thrilled!

When I got home from school, the first thing I did was to hunt down my mom so I could get her permission to go.

"Mom, can I go to a party Saturday night with my boyfriend?"

"Where is it going to be?" she asked.

"In McHenry."

"At whose house?"

"One of his friend's. I'm not sure what his name is."

"Who else is going?"

"I don't know," I answered. "I didn't ask."

She looked me in the eyes and said simply, "No."

"No!" I shouted. "Why not?"

"Because I said so."

She always used that remark to close a discussion. I was never satisfied with it, but this time I wanted a real reason. I was very irritated.

"Why not?" I pressed. "The boys get to go to parties. I ask once and you say no. Now, why not?"

"I have my reasons," she said.

"Well, what are they?" I kept pestering her, hoping I could do a little bargaining. She just kept looking at me and then said firmly, "I said NO and that's final!"

I was extremely upset. The next day at school, I told my boyfriend I couldn't go with him. When he asked why, I felt embarrassed when I said, "My mother won't let me."

"Sneak, then," he advised.

"Yeah, I could do that."

We devised a plan I knew would work.

Saturday morning came, and as I did my weekly household chores, I kept looking at Mom. She looked bedraggled. She and Dad had had a terrific upset the night before and every time I looked at her I wanted to cry. She obviously hadn't slept much and I could see weariness and pain written all over her face. I wanted badly to have a heart-to-heart talk with her. I felt she needed a friend, and I wanted to be that friend. I really cared about her and Dad, but the barriers between us seemed unsurmountable. I kept thinking about the party that night. My boyfriend was going to call to make sure everything was still set with our plan.

At noon, the phone rang. It was for me. "Hi. Are you all set for the big party tonight?" I hesitated for a moment, then swallowed hard. "I've changed my mind. I'm not going."

"What?" he blurted out. "Why not?"

"I'm just not in the mood to party, I guess."

"Oh, come on, Deb! You're not going to let your old lady run your life, are you?"

I hated it when my peers called their parents "old man" or "old lady." Even when I thought my parents were a little off on some things, I never spoke about them that way. It made me cringe. The conversation continued and the pressure increased. He wasn't going to take no for an answer, and I wasn't about to budge, either. I thought, "All Mom needs after last night is a rebellious teenager on her hands." Even though I didn't understand her reasons for not letting me go, I felt I needed to respect her decision. All I knew was that I loved her and I wanted to please her.

"She's ruining your life!" he persisted.

"Look," I said firmly, "I've decided I'm not going and I'm not changing my mind. No one is going to ruin my life, including you. Now, if you want to go, fine, but count me out. I'm sorry!" With that, I heard him slam the telephone receiver down.

I was quiet all evening and kept to myself. Mom was quiet, too. We exchanged some small talk, but most of the time passed in silence. I was depressed and, I think I'm safe in saying, she was too.

On Monday morning, when I arrived at school, a friend came running down the hall towards my locker. She was yelling, "Deb, Deb, did you hear?"

"Hear what?" I asked, looking puzzled.

"You didn't hear yet? The party you were supposed to go to Saturday night got busted!"

I stared. "No, you're kidding."

"No, I'm not. The cops evidently hauled several people in for smoking pot and drinking. I guess it was a real mess."

"Wow!" I said. "Thanks for the info. Gotta run. I'll catch ya later." The bell was about to ring, so I hurried to my first class.

All I could think about was how I had given my mom such a hassle for not letting me go. Now I felt awful about it. I knew that my date smoked pot, but I never expected him to get caught. I was so thankful I had changed my mind.

That same day, at lunch, I got dumped. I was informed that my boyfriend had met someone else who was "more his type" at the party. I was disappointed, but I understood. I suspected it was best.

My journals grew by leaps and bounds in high school. It was the only way I could clearly sort out my feelings and keep myself feeling upbeat.

At this point in time, my heart condition didn't challenge me much physically. Sure, my activities were still limited, but I understood my boundaries and paced myself accordingly. Overall, I felt great and was thrilled with my progress.

Emotionally I still had many set backs. I was at an age where make-up worked wonderfully. I hid my purple lips under lipstick and nail polish worked great for the finger nails. Rouge added some color to my pale face, but I still wasn't naturally pretty like other girls my age. Many times I felt worthless and depressed. I often wanted to run away and die. I asked myself, "Why do I have to be different and why do I have to be the one with a heart disease?" I knew deep inside that others still saw it as a problem, especially the guys. Some shied away, others made cruel remarks. I wondered daily if I would ever feel special.

Mom used to come in my room at night to see what I was doing. I spent hours in there with the door shut, just trying to block the depression from my mind.

Sometimes I tried to read my Bible. I received it in Sunday school when I was seven years old, but we hadn't been to church since then, so I always got totally lost before I got through the book of Genesis. I then placed it back on the shelf where it collected dust for another year.

One evening I was invited out with some friends. We planned to go disco dancing, but we couldn't get in because we were too young. Instead we found a way to buy a twelve pack of beer. As we drank and hollered, we raced down the dark country roads, laughing and throwing the beer cans out the windows. A couple of the girls got drunk. By that time the smell of the beer was making me sick, so I decided not to drink anymore that night. When I got home, I was relieved to see Mom was already in bed. I knew if she smelled beer on my breath she would be furious! Dad probably wouldn't have cared. What could he say, anyway?

As I got ready for bed, I thought about my dad. All it takes is one beer and who knows where it can go from there? As much as I always wanted to be a part of the crowd, I suddenly realized that it wasn't worth it.

Seances and Ouija board games with my friends were horrifying and definitely unsatisfying. I felt extremely frustrated and lonely. I was desperately searching for something more, but I couldn't seem to put my finger on it.

Several weeks later, I needed a ride to work and some classmates from my English class offered to take me. No sooner were we out of the parking lot when out came the joints. They offered me one and I said, "Sure!" I had never been around marijuana. Perhaps this was what I was looking for. As I started to put the joint to my lips, my mind started thinking, "Deb, this is illegal. If you get caught, you'll be dead meat! You'll probably lose your job and, if nothing else, your heart won't like it and you'll end up sick. Then this whole carload of peers will end up in trouble."

Everyone kept on encouraging me, "Come on, Deb. Give it a try. You'll like it."

"Yes, that's what I'm afraid of," I answered. I realized it was easier to quit now, before I even started. I handed the joint back to someone and said, "Not today."

One other time I literally climbed out of a car window in a skirt because I felt I was being forced to try drugs. I could see how substance abuse was destroying my family, and I chose not to get myself involved in something like that.

One summer during my junior high years, our dear neighbor Mrs. Scherer hired me to plant and take care of her flower beds. Besides enjoying the extra spending money, I discovered that I really enjoyed gardening. I continued to work for her each summer. I felt so special when Mrs. Scherer took me to breakfast and then to the local nursery to help her select the flowers for her summer gardens.

As high school freshmen, we were required to research and write a vocational notebook. In it we were to describe about all the aspects of a career of our choice. While growing up, I always dreamed of being a nurse. As I thought about writing my notebook, I realized nursing would be impossible for me since I had become very queasy around blood. I had no idea what to write about.

One day while I was over at Mrs. Scherer's house I explained my dilemma to her and asked for any suggestions. We talked for some time and then she suggested that since I enjoyed gardening so much, was creative, and worked well with my hands, perhaps a greenhouse or flower shop job might be suitable for me. That idea had never even crossed my mind. I decided to do my report on being a floral designer.

Ready and excited for my high school Senior Prom

Those awkward stages of adolescence — Searching for my identity

IV

Fairy Tale Prince

It was March 11, of my senior year. I went through the lunch line with my fifty cents and bought my usual hot pretzel, ice cream sandwich, and carton of chocolate milk. Then, wandering through the cafeteria, I looked for my friends. I noticed that there weren't enough chairs at their table, so I set down my tray and turned to look for one. A guy sitting across the table jumped up and said, "Hi, may I find a chair for you?"

I blushed as I answered, "Sure if you would like to."

He quickly returned with the chair and helped me get seated. As he walked over to the other side of the table, I whispered to my friend, "Is he new here? I don't remember seeing him before."

"No," she laughed. "Let me introduce you." His name was Tom.

"Do you always eat such a strange lunch?" he asked. I blushed again as we began to exchange small talk.

Since I was a part of the school work program, I did not have time to linger over lunch. I was now working at a local florist and greenhouse. My bosses, Joan and Bernie, would be waiting for me and I didn't want to let them down. They were always so good to me. I was walking to work that day and needed at least a half hour to get there. I said good-bye to my friends and went to dump my garbage. As I stood at the trash barrel, a shadow came up behind me.

"It's me again," a voice said. "Can I walk with you to work?" It was Tom. "I can only walk partway because I have a class in a little while."

I smiled and said, "Sure! I'd like your company. We'd better get going."

I was so impressed that I could hardly look at him. I thought I must be dreaming and would surely wake up at any moment. During our walk, he did most of the talking. He was different than most guys I knew -- very polite and a lot of fun to be with. My feet hardly touched the ground the whole way to work. The next day he asked me to go out Saturday night. I could hardly believe that a guy I liked was also interested in me. Other boys had not treated me like I was someone special. Once in a while I was asked to go on a blind date, or was asked out by a "nerd," but I was good at saying, "I'm sorry. I already have plans for that evening." Those plans usually meant baby-sitting, writing letters, or sewing. This was different.

Saturday night Tom arrived on time with a vase of flowers. I was so surprised and pleased. They were beautiful! I felt like a queen.

As the months passed, we continued dating. He asked me to my Senior Prom. Mom sewed my dress for me in pink and white. Bernie let me make Tom's pink rose boutonniere. The night was perfect. Before we left the dance, we took a walk, hand in hand, under the moonlit sky. As the breeze blew softly through my hair, Tom asked me to go steady. He gave me a beautiful gold bracelet, engraved with my name on the front and the date and my nickname on the back. I couldn't wait to get home and tell my family.

Unfortunately, things at home were still not good. There was constant turmoil. I wanted to share more of my life with my mother, but a barrier had developed between us. Mom gave me the impression that she expected perfectionism from me, like she did herself. I often felt like a failure because I couldn't meet all of her expectations. No matter how hard I tried, there was always something wrong. I found it extremely difficult to be a "perfect" daughter. It seemed like she was hesitant to share my happiness about Tom also. When I tried to warm up to her, she often snapped at me or changed the subject. I, in turn, withdrew and seldom went into much detail about what was happening in my life. We shared small talk, but that was about all at this point.

Mom spent that summer up at a Girl Scout camp in Wisconsin to earn money for the family. Dad was seldom home. If, by chance, he did show up sober, he helped me prepare the evening meal. While he cooked the meat on the grill, I set the table and finished the rest of the meal. At those times, Dad was easy to talk to. After dinner I made a special effort to sit and visit with him for awhile, but he often drank while we were talking and that upset me.

During that summer I struggled with a big decision. I was looking forward to going to the local junior college in the fall, but money was tight. Besides tuition and books, I needed a car, insurance, and gas. I had been saving for quite a while, but it wasn't enough.

I asked Bernie, my boss, if I could have a raise, at least to minimum wage. He looked at me very sadly as he said, "I'm sorry. You deserve it, but financially I can't do it right now."

I loved Joan and Bernie. They were so kind to me. They never forgot to ask how my day was going or how I was feeling. They supplied me with the hugs and compliments that were missing at home. Bernie was like a father to me through my junior and senior years of high school. I remember how upset he was when I hitchhiked to work one cold winter day. He insisted that if I ever needed a ride again, I should call him. He was extremely patient as I struggled to learn floral designing. He never yelled at me when I made a mistake, even when I fell through the bench in the greenhouse and left an awful mess of dirt, broken plants, and flowerpots.

But now I had to decide if I could afford to stay, or if I had to leave. I hated the decision pressed upon me. I struggled for weeks, but when it came to the bottom line, I had to choose between my present job and college. I cried as I wrote my letter of resignation.

When fall arrived, I was still seeing Tom as often as possible. His positive attitude and caring personality helped me become more bubbly and confident. For the first time in my life, I felt special. I was eager to begin working for my degree in ornamental horticulture and floral design.

On my way to my first day of work at my new job, working in another floral shop, someone ran a red light and plowed into my car. The next thing I knew, I was being rushed to the hospital in an ambulance. I kept thinking, "Lord, please don't let there be a death involved. Don't let me lose my job. And, help Grandpa not to be upset with me." Grandpa had been so good about helping me choose and finance the car--and now it was ruined.

While the doctor bandaged my cut arm and reset my dislocated thumb, Mom called my new boss to explain why I had not arrived. My head throbbed with pain as a result of hitting the rear view mirror, which in turn broke the windshield. I felt awful.

When we got home, Mom was upset with me because the accident would increase our insurance rates. I tried to explain that it wasn't my fault. I wanted to shout at her, "Aren't you glad I'm alive? Besides, I pay the insurance!" But I didn't say a word. I knew deep down that she was glad I was okay. I simply swallowed hard, turned my face away, and went to my room.

I was relieved when the police came to the door with the accident report and my driver's license. They confirmed that it wasn't my fault. I didn't even get a ticket. The only other injury in the accident was a sprained ankle of a passenger in the other car. And Grandpa was very understanding.

I returned to college the following week, bandages and all. My grades were up, I had met several new friends, and I was often asked out by really nice guys. But I always replied with a smile, "Sorry. I have a steady."

My new job, on the other hand, was a struggle. My boss was not at all like Joan or Bernie. She was more like a drill sergeant, always parading around acting irritated. She was very impersonal with her employees and I was afraid to be near her. I began to dread going to work, but I needed the money. I tried to go in each day wearing a smile and with a positive attitude, but I often left feeling defeated!

Tom and I were growing in love each day. We went out together or talked on the phone every night. On weekends we sometimes worked on his car. He taught me how to drive his sister's motorcycle, and he always got excited when he told me about the one he was saving money for. That December we shared a memorable Christmas together, and then, in no time, we were into summer vacation again.

The day we spent together at the county fair was glorious. Afterward we shared an intimate dinner, and then went for a stroll along the river in the moonlight. It was there that he got down on his knee and proposed to me. Of course I said, "Yes!" Then he slipped a lovely heart-shaped diamond ring onto my finger. I was so happy! It felt good to be loved. I wanted to tell everyone I knew. But when I got home, the house was quiet. My dad and brothers were asleep and Mom was at scout camp. There was no one to tell.

When Mom did return from camp, she was in no mood to share my joy. I was hurt and angered by her response. While she was off at camp, I had been the mother and maid of the household. After my full day at work, not only had I kept the house clean, but did the laundry, fixed the meals, took care of my youngest brother -- including supporting him at all of his baseball games, shopped for groceries, went to the bank with the remnants of Dad's paycheck, paid some of the bills, and, worst of all, put up with all of Dad's nonsense. Now Mom was upset with me because there was no money for a wedding. I assured her it didn't have to be big or fancy. All I wanted was to be happy with Tom. Evidently she was unable to see beyond her own misery.

By the following spring, the plans for our October wedding were moving along. The bridesmaids' dresses and wedding invitations were picked out, I was making monthly payments on my bridal gown, the cake had been ordered, the church was reserved, and I had purchased silk flowers so I could begin arranging them at home in my spare time. Everything was going smoothly!

Tom and I took a trip to Chicago where I had my yearly heart check-up with my specialist, Dr. Cole. He explained to Tom how risky it would be for me to have a baby. He strongly advised that we use precautions and that we consider adoption as a safer alternative. We discussed it all on the way home. Tom was very understanding.

In May I graduated from college with honors and an award of

excellence in floral design. I was thrilled to have successfully reached my goal. Things were somewhat better at work. Tom kept encouraging me to look around, but I knew that once we were married, this job would be close to our new home and I liked that convenience. So I hung in there.

In June we began our premarital counseling sessions with the minister who was going to marry us. Neither one of us were members of any church, so it was awkward.

Then suddenly, Tom became withdrawn and cool. I had never seen him act this way before. I kept asking him about it, but he kept saying nothing was wrong. I didn't trust his answers.

With less than three months until our wedding, Tom shocked me with the truth. He finally admitted that, at this point in time, he felt uncomfortable about such a big commitment. Besides, he told me, he wanted to buy his motorcycle first. He suggested that we both date around a little bit before tying the knot. I was sure Tom was the man for me, but evidently he was not so sure about me. He wanted to postpone the wedding, at least for a little while.

I was devastated! "Lord," I cried, "if you are really up there, why are you doing this to me?" The one thing in my life I thought was perfect had just dumped on me! My Prince Charming was turning into a toad and I didn't know how to break the spell! What happened to our "happily ever after" ending? Where was my fairy godmother when I needed her?

V

Escape Into Darkness

It was a summer evening shortly after Tom and I broke up. My older brother was out with his buddies, my younger brother was with his girlfriend, and my youngest brother was asleep. I had just hung up the phone from talking with Mom. She was at scout camp again and usually called several times each week to see how things were going at home.

As I walked down the hallway from the kitchen, I saw headlights through the front windows. I recognized the sound of the vehicle. It was Dad's truck, even later than usual. I hurried to my room. I knew what shape he would be in and I didn't want to greet him. I heard him stumble through the back door as I prepared for bed. Usually he just plopped down on the sofa and fell asleep. That night, I heard him shuffle down the hall toward the bedrooms. When he saw my light shining under the door, he poked his head in and slurred, "H-i, D-e-b-b-i-e!"

"Hi," I answered abruptly, trying to cut him short. He came toward me, reeking of alcohol and cigarette smoke. I didn't need to look at him to know that his eyes were bloodshot.

"I want a kissh!" he demanded.

"No!" I answered. "Now get out of my room." I began to shake.

"Debbie, thish ish your daddy," he slurred, "and I want a kissh." He laughed in an evil tone.

"No!" I snapped back once again. "Now get out of my room, right now!"

He refused. I yelled, "You stink! You're drunk! And I think you're a jerk! Now leave me alone! I hate you!"

Dad often asked me for a kiss when he was drunk, but his persistence that night, made me panic. I knew I was in trouble when he grabbed my arm and pulled me toward him. His forceful arms were around me and he started to kiss me. I pushed his face away. I didn't have a moment to waste. I had to think fast!

"Dad," I asked, "have you eaten dinner yet?"

He stopped, thought for a minute, and answered, "No!"

"Oh, well," I replied, "you better grab a bite to eat. You must be starving. There are leftovers in the refrigerator and some cake on the counter. Go help yourself."

He turned away and stumbled down the hallway toward the kitchen, tripping over his own feet. I quickly closed my door and, using all my meager strength, pushed my biggest dresser in front of it. Then I sat down on my bed, tears streaming down my face. I smelled food burning in the kitchen, but I wasn't about to go help. I just hoped Dad didn't burn the house down.

And where was Mom when I needed her? At camp! I resented her for leaving us, weeks at a time, and now I was angry. My teenage life was changing drastically and I needed her love more now than ever before.

How badly I wanted to call Tom. We had been so close. Why was our relationship now miles apart? I still loved him and that night I needed his help. But I had no one. I was alone again and scared stiff.

Gradually I began to calm down. The kitchen became quiet so I assumed that Dad had finally gone to sleep. I turned off my light and began to doze off. Suddenly, "Bang! Bang! Bang!" Someone was pounding on my door. I sat bolt upright in bed, my heart instantly pounding all over again. "Oh, no," I thought. "He's back."

"Let me in!" he ordered. "I want a kissh!"

“Oh, Lord,” I prayed, “if you are really up there, please help me!” I watched in horror as the door and dresser started to move. Light from the hallway pierced the darkness of my room. I saw him silhouetted against the light as the door slowly opened.

“What do I do now?” I wondered.

In desperation, I feverishly planned my escape. My only way out was into darkness. If I kicked the screen off the window, I could clamber through the opening. Maybe I could run to a neighbor’s house. I needed help. But, no, that wouldn’t work. By this time it was extremely late and all of the houses were dark. Besides, I was in my night shirt. There was still hope. I could easily hide underneath the lilac bush beside my window. But what about my sleeping brother? I was afraid to leave him inside the house. But did I have any other choice?

Once outside, my only hope of getting back in would be to wait in the darkness until my drunk father went to sleep. Then I could tiptoe cautiously past him as he slept on the sofa in front of the television. I had done that numerous times before.

Dad’s voice interrupted my thoughts. “Where did that dumb kid go?” he mumbled.

Weeks later, Mom questioned me about my torn screen. I made some excuse. I knew I needed to start looking for a place of my own. I could not deal with the stress of living at home any longer.

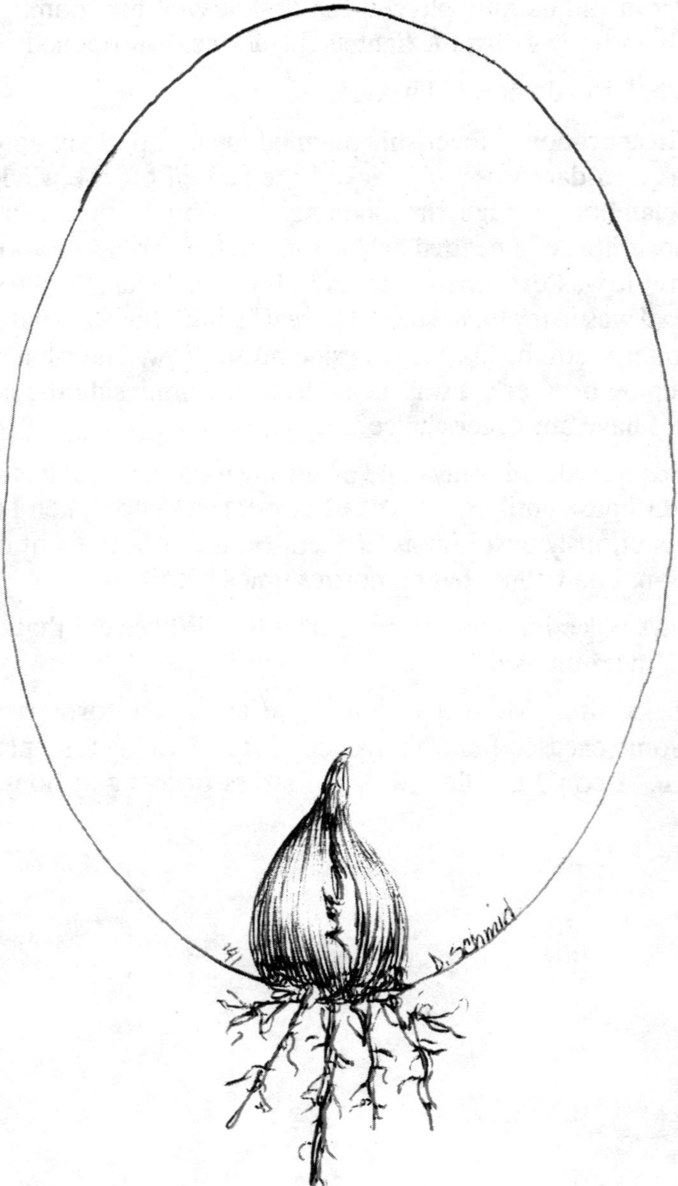

VI

Torn Between Two

"Telephone, Deb!" came the summons one evening in August.

"Who is it?" I asked.

"I'm not sure. It's some guy," my brother replied.

"Is it Tom?"

"No. Just answer the phone!"

I put the phone to my ear. "Hello."

"Hello, Debbie? This is Tom from a flower shop in Woodstock." Just the name "Tom" made my heart race. "You remember Gloria from college? Well, I'm the manager here and we're looking for a floral designer. She highly recommended you. I thought perhaps you would be interested in applying for the position."

"That's considerate of her to recommend me," I said, "but I am currently employed at a florist in McHenry."

"I know you are," he answered, "but Gloria mentioned that you were not very happy there. Is that true?"

"Well, yes. In some ways I feel I could be happier elsewhere, but I don't know what to say right now. May I think about it tonight and call you back tomorrow?" I jotted down his phone number.

After I hung up, Mom and I discussed the possibility of a job change. I was getting along better with my boss now, because I understood some of her moods. Also I had just received a raise and I wasn't anxious to drop back down to minimum wage again.

On the other hand, it wouldn't hurt to apply for the job. Even if I decided later not to take it, the interview itself would be good experience.

The next evening I called the manager of the Woodstock flower shop. He had given me his home phone number since he knew I would be returning his call after work hours. A woman answered. She sounded hurried and uncomfortable as she explained that Tom was not home yet. She said she would tell him I had called.

Not long after, the phone rang. It was Tom. I apologized for disturbing his wife with my call. He laughed. "That wasn't my wife. My mother is here visiting for a few days." I felt so stupid! I agreed to accept the interview with him and we set a time.

On the day of the interview, I worked at the flower shop in McHenry all day, then went straight to Woodstock. As I opened the door to the store, I was greeted by a dark headed, over six-foot-tall, young man.

"Hi, are you Tom?" I asked.

"Yes," he replied with a smile. "Come on in."

I filled out the application and then he interviewed me. I felt very relaxed until he mentioned my engagement ring. When he asked about my wedding plans, I just smiled and told him that the wedding had been postponed and I wasn't sure when another date would be set. Then he asked me to come back again to do some designing for the owners. I agreed.

The following week I gave my boss two weeks' notice. She seemed very disappointed but wished me luck. As I started to walk away, she said, "Debbie, I usually don't tell anyone this, but you have been an excellent employee. If you ever want to come back, please let me know."

Monday, September 10, I began to work at the flower shop in Woodstock. I was a little nervous, but the morning went quickly. I worked with Tom and he explained all the store policies and procedures. After lunch I was able to do some work in the design room. Gloria was also working that day. It was fun to see her again. As we worked and talked, Tom sat in his office nearby with his door open, doing paperwork. When Gloria asked me how my wedding plans were coming, I shocked her by showing her my ringless finger and telling her it was off. At first, she thought I was kidding. When I told her I wished I were, she started to cry as she hugged me.

"He meant the world to you, Deb!" she commiserated.

"I know," I answered with a lump in my throat. "Things in life change, I guess. Gloria, I'm convinced, life is full of nothing but pain and broken promises." I hurriedly changed the subject. The mention of Tom made me choke up and often brought me to tears.

Tuesday evening, when Mom and I returned from some shopping, I was surprised to find a message on the counter from my younger brother. It read, "Deb, call Tom from the flower shop in Woodstock when you get home. O-O-O!"

"Uh, oh," I thought. Reluctantly I returned his call. "What did I do wrong?" I asked.

"Oh, Deb, this call has nothing to do with work. Besides, you are doing just fine." He went on to explain that he had overheard my conversation with Gloria the day before and he was wondering if I would go out to dinner with him.

"I'm not sure. Can I think about it and let you know tomorrow?" I asked. He told me to call him in the morning. Wednesday was his day off so he planned to be at home. After I hung up, I almost jumped for joy.

"What was that all about?" Mom asked. I explained.

"I told him I needed to think about it. I don't want to look too anxious, you know!" I knew all along that my answer was yes.

I felt a little awkward accepting dates with other guys, especially one of my bosses, but we had a nice time. I was impressed with his manner and the fact that he treated me like a lady. We decided it would be best if we did not tell anyone at work about our date. There wasn't any sense in starting gossip.

During the next several months, I dated Tom off and on. Many times I felt like he was smothering me and I backed away. I also talked on the phone with other guys I had met in college. Several asked me out, but I wasn't interested. I didn't trust anyone at this point and I definitely wasn't ready to make any major decisions about guys. Besides, I still talked to the old Tom occasionally. My love for him burned even yet, so I refused to completely give up on him. Weeks passed where I did not see or talk to the old Tom, but it never failed, whenever I was with my boss, he called or popped in.

Occasionally my phone messages read, "Deb, call Tom."

"Tom who?" I asked. "Tom, Tom," kept ringing in my ears! We had "Old Tom," "New Tom," "Tom from work," "Tom from Woodstock," "Tall Tom," and "Short Tom." Finally, I became so confused I didn't know which Tom was which. One night I said, "Okay, everyone! From now on, let's call the new Tom just plain 'Tom.' The old Tom, we will call 'Walley'!" Everyone agreed and things became much easier.

For several months I searched for an apartment, but financially, I couldn't swing it. My co-worker, Gloria, knew about my dilemma and asked me if I would be interested in sub-leasing their apartment. Her husband was pursuing his college education and it required them to live in Mississippi from January through May.

I thought it was a wonderful idea. Not only would it give me a chance to be out on my own, but it would also provide the opportunity to sort out my feelings about the two Toms, without the added stress of living at home.

Mom watched while I carefully packed my things. The look on her face was unforgettable, as she stood by the front door and waved good-bye . Even though I was only moving a half hour away, suddenly it felt like I was going half way around the world. As much as I hated the situation at home, I felt sorry for those I was leaving behind. I knew I was going to be relieved from sleepless nights and fights, but those I loved would still suffer.

On Valentine's Day, Tom gave me a small, beautifully wrapped package. The minute he gave it to me, I became uncomfortable. I knew he was much more serious about me than I was about him. I opened it slowly and carefully. I was relieved to find a lovely necklace and not a ring.

"It's precious, Tom," I said. I smiled as he helped me put it on, and thanked him for his thoughtfulness. He leaned over and gave me a kiss. "There's something special I've been wanting to ask you for quite some time now."

"Oh no," I thought. "Here goes!"

"What's that?" I asked hesitantly.

With all the sincerity in the world, he asked, "Will you marry me?"

My heart sank to my stomach as I gazed up at him. Instantly a lump formed in my throat and tears filled my eyes. I could hardly find the words to answer him. "I'm sorry, Tom, but I just can't accept your proposal right now. I'm not ready to make that kind of commitment." I told him I cared about him, but I asked him to please try to understand. His brown eyes were full of sadness. It was obvious he was very disappointed.

I started to cry. I didn't know what else to say or do. I suddenly realized I had been unfair to him and I felt awful. I started to take off the necklace. He stopped me. "Please, Deb, keep the necklace."

"I can't."

"Forget the proposal," he pleaded. "Please just wear the necklace and know that I care about you, okay?"

Reluctantly, I agreed.

"Will you keep seeing me?" he asked.

After a long silence, I answered, "If you want to, but I'm not sure I'm the girl you deserve." He looked puzzled. "Why not?"

"Just because," I answered.

He kept looking at me as I sat silently. Finally he broke the silence. "Deb, you must have some reason for saying that. Now, what is it?"

"I do have a reason, but I prefer not to talk about it tonight, okay?"

There was no way he was willing to accept that answer. He wanted to know the reason, and he wanted to know that night. He had incredible patience and he was willing to wait however long it would take me to get it out. It was so difficult for me to talk. I always dealt with crisis alone. How could I share my feelings with Tom? Could I really trust this guy? Or, would I just be setting myself up for more pain?

After about an hour, I finally said, "You're right, Tom. You deserve an answer." I looked down at the floor, feeling totally embarrassed. Through my tears I said "Tom, I have not told anyone this before, so please keep it to yourself." He promised and encouraged me to continue. My tears seemed endless as I told him I was no longer a virgin. Even though my family had not attended church for several years, I had been raised to be moral. I had waited for the one I was going to marry. However, he had backed out after I had given in. I knew only too well now that I should have waited until after the "I do" before saying "I will." But now it was too late. What was done was done.

Tom gave me a tissue and quietly put his arm around me. He kissed me on the forehead. The room was dreadfully silent. The only sounds were my sobs.

As he drove me to my apartment, we were both very quiet. He kissed me good night and told me that he still loved me. I hugged him and whispered "Thank you" and "Goodnight."

On April 23, I invited Tom over to my place for dinner. It was his birthday and I wanted to fix him something homemade. As we sat down to eat, the phone rang. It was Walley. I hadn't heard from him in months. Now he was telling me he wanted to see me again. Why now? Poor Tom sat patiently at the table as I talked on the phone and dinner got cold.

When Walley came by a few days later, I felt nervous. I had never felt that way with him before, not even on our first date. The worst of it was that he knew me so well I couldn't hide it from him.

"Deb, why are you biting your fingernails?" he teased. "You aren't nervous, are you?" He was the same old Tom I had loved dearly, but conversation was awkward. He told me he missed me and that girls like me were hard to find. I wanted to believe him, but I wasn't sure what to think. If I was so special to him, why had he just asked me again for his ring and stereo? Did he want me back or out of his life forever? I was so confused.

As Walley and I were standing in the front foyer saying goodnight, I noticed that Tom drove by twice. Each time, when he saw Walley's Datsun, he drove on. Walley and I gave each other a hug and kiss good-bye but I felt uncomfortable. We had been apart for over nine months and our relationship now felt awkward and unfamiliar.

As I lay in bed that night, I realized how very important the evening had been. In spite of the fact that I missed so many things about Walley, I now realized I had changed while we were apart. For one thing, I wasn't as wild or immature. Under Tom's gentle attention, I had cleaned up my speech and begun to act more like a young lady. I was afraid that if I waited much longer for Walley, Tom might slip away and perhaps I would end up losing both of them. I decided I needed to give Tom a fair chance. We needed to pursue our relationship out from under Walley's shadow. Tom's patience, understanding, and tenderness were winning my heart.

On May 26, at sunset, Tom and I walked along the beach. As we stood holding hands, watching the ducks swimming by, Tom bent over and kissed me as he asked again, "Now, will you marry me?"

This time I hugged him and said, "Yes, I would love to!" I was finally willing to put the past behind me and looked forward to happiness with Tom.

However, at times there were setbacks. One summer evening Tom and I had just sat down to dinner, at my parents house, when Walley knocked on the door. I was shocked. Several months had passed with no word from him. Why now? I stepped outside to talk for a minute. After a brief visit, he looked at Tom's car in the drive and said, "Guess I better let you go. Looks like you already have company." He began walking away, then turned and reminded me, "By the way, you still have my ring and stereo."

Later that evening, when I was sitting at my desk, Mom came into my room and sat down on my bed. I moved back home because my sub-lease on the apartment was over and I hadn't located a new place yet. I was hoping to have a good mother/daughter talk. Instead, she said, "Debbie, I don't think you're being fair to Tom."

I turned quickly. "What?"

"You heard me," she replied. "I think you're playing games with him."

I couldn't believe what I was hearing. Didn't she know I was hurting? "Mom," I answered defensively, "you obviously don't understand what I'm going through!"

"Yes, I do," she replied.

"How can you? I don't even understand. I can't believe you think I'm playing games! I didn't call Walley. He came over." I wanted so badly to explain my intense pain to Mom, but the lump in my throat made it impossible for me to speak.

She looked at me as if she were disappointed in what she heard, then left the room.

"Please don't leave my room in silence, Mom," I thought. "Can't you see my tears? Please help me understand my pain." But she had her own pain to deal with. Her relationship with Dad was the pits, and, although I didn't understand at the time, we were both hurting in similar ways. We were both silently struggling with losing someone we had loved. Once again I sat alone to sort through my life with journal and pen.

It had been well over a year since Walley had called off our wedding, but I was still trying to figure out what happened between us. Even though I had decided to pursue a relationship with Tom, my heart longed for understanding. What had happened a year ago that turned him away so suddenly? Was it something I said or did? Was it my heart condition that bothered him? Maybe if I had only been healthier, prettier, or more athletic, he would have been happier. Everything always seemed to be my fault. How I longed to understand. I felt responsible for this whole upset. Would I ever find out, or would I only guess and blame myself forever?

Tom and I — Just clowning around!

New Beginnings

Our Special Day
October 25

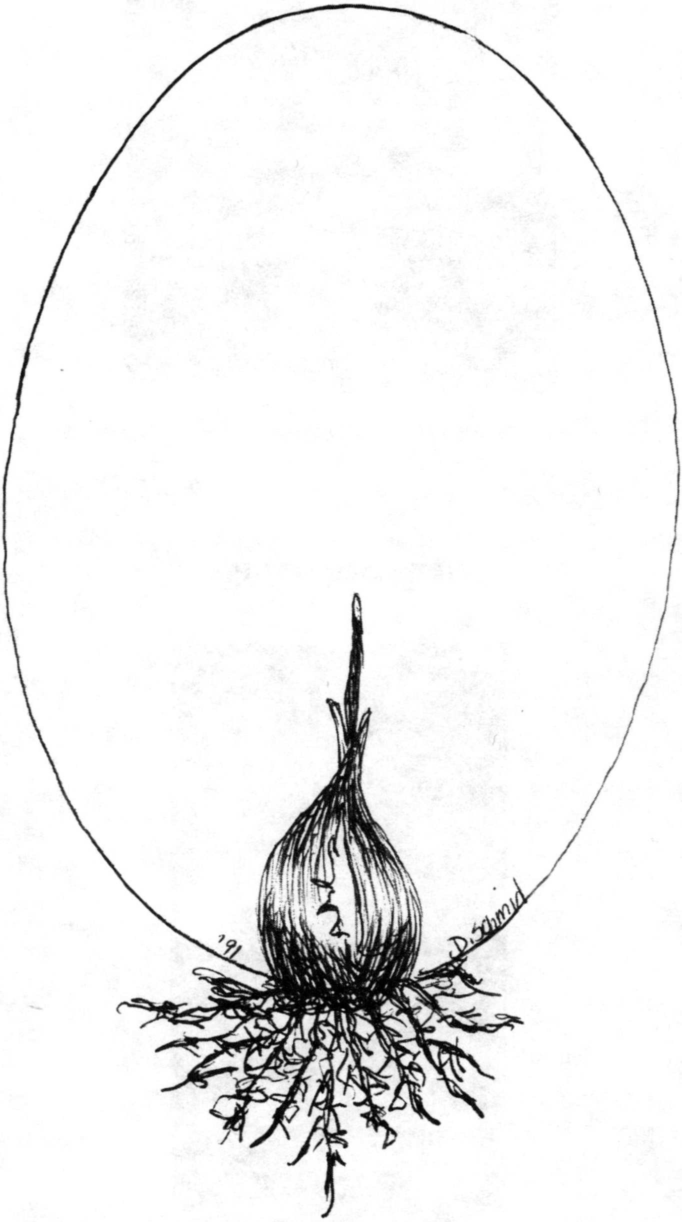
'91
D. Schmid

VII

New Beginnings

The priest was trying hard to be patient, but I was not cooperating. All he wanted was my signature on a piece of paper stating that I would use no birth control except natural methods, but I was being stubborn.

One more time he reviewed the scriptures that said to be fruitful and multiply.

"That's fine," I said, "for someone strong and healthy, but it's not fine for me. With my heart problems, there would be great risk both to me and the baby if I became pregnant."

"God is the giver and taker of life," the priest explained. "If he wants you to die in childbirth, you should accept His will."

"That's stupid," I snapped. "He's also the giver of common sense and I think He expects us to use it."

Tom sat quietly. This was his church, not mine. He wouldn't argue with the priest, but he didn't try to argue with me either. In fact, we had already discussed the method of birth control we intended to use. I could not bring myself to sign that paper, knowing I had no intention of abiding by it. The priest could not hide his shock when I handed the paper back to him unsigned.

"If you don't sign this," he warned, "I can't marry you."

"That's fine," I shot back. "But I'm not a liar."

All the way back to the car, I angrily re-hashed all my arguments with Tom who tried to calm me with his usual, unruffled manner. I got into the car, slammed the door, and turned my face away from him. I was close to tears. I thought the priest and the Catholic Church were being very unfair.

Tom eventually persuaded me to continue attending our premarital counseling sessions, including six weeks of classes on natural birth control. However, by the last session, I still had not signed the required paper. We had all our other papers in order, including the signatures of four people who had known me all my life and were willing to confirm that I was not pregnant. The only thing that now stood in the way of us getting married was my signature.

Finally, just before that last session, I thought of a solution. "Okay, I'll go and sign it," I told Tom. "And I'll be completely honest. You don't have to sign anything saying you won't use birth control, so you get to be the one who wears it!" He gave me a relieved smile and hug, and off we went to our final class.

The evening before our wedding was unseasonably cold and damp. The wind was brisk and whistled through the car as my bridesmaids and I drove home from the rehearsal dinner. My friends teased me about the possibility of having to wear my long underwear under my bridal gown. We were laughing and carrying on like a bunch of school girls. Suddenly Kim, who was driving, said, "Oh-oh, there's something wrong with this car." We pulled over to the side of the dark country road and got out. The three of us stood in skirts and high heels, looking under the hood, trying to decide what to do. Kim had been having minor problems with the car, but this was different. No matter what we did, we couldn't get it going. I had learned a lot about car engines when I helped Walley rebuild his Datsun, but I couldn't find the problem either.

Not a soul had passed us since we broke down. We decided that instead of standing there freezing, we should start walking toward my house. It was only a little more than a mile away, but my friends were concerned about me. I was already shivering and my lips were purple from the cold. We could see one or two lonely farm houses, but since it was so late, they were dark. As we were locking up the car, a Jeep drove past. Being left behind, we felt more alone than ever. Suddenly, its brake lights came on, it turned and came back to our car. The driver stopped and rolled down the window.

"Hey! Are you girls having car trouble?" We told him we had no idea what the problem was. He jumped out of the Jeep and fiddled under the hood for a few minutes, but without success. "Where are you headed?" he asked. We told him. "That's not far. Hop in."

We were reluctant to get into a vehicle with a strange guy, but since there were three of us and (we assumed) only one of him, we agreed. By this time I was really cold and needed to get to a warm place fast. We all climbed into the Jeep, and were surprised to discover two more guys inside. Suddenly we became a little nervous. The guys invited us to go out for pizza with them but we declined. They thought we were kidding when we said I was getting married in the morning. I looked very young.

"Boy, I've heard all kinds of lines from girls," one of them commented, "but this one tops them all!"

We were relieved when they took us right to my parents' house. We thanked them and, as we got out of the car, Kim reached for what she thought was her purse. Instead, she squeezed one of the guys' knees! We giggled as we walked in the front door.

Kim and my dear friend, Tammy, spent the night at my house and we reminisced about old times at this last slumber party. But, even after the talk died down, I had trouble getting to sleep. I was too excited about the next morning.

I had always dreamed of having an evening candlelight wedding, but I also wanted my dad to walk me down the aisle. I knew the chances were better for him to be sober in the morning, so morning it was. The date we set was October 25 and Dad arrived at the wedding in perfect shape. As the music started and I saw my bridesmaids begin to walk down the aisle, the butterflies in my stomach started to flutter at double speed. Deep inside I still thought Tom was too good for me. I didn't deserve a guy like him. I smiled at Dad and said, "Well, I guess this is it." He hugged me, gave me a kiss, and told me he loved me. Then "Edelweiss" began to play. I was bursting with joy as my dad took my hand and we started down the aisle. I could see Tom waiting for me at the front of the church, his face beaming with happiness. We were soon going to be man and wife.

Now that we were married, the atmosphere at work became quite stressful. Although I was one of the main floral designers, now that I was the manager's wife, I found myself even more isolated from the other employees. Since I was not in a management position either, I didn't fit in anywhere. Some days were pretty rough, but I plugged along and tried to keep my smile. Tom had hopes of buying the business someday, so it was important for me to hang in there.

After several months I was given a little bit of authority and my fellow employees resented it. One lady in particular became an irritation. She enjoyed stirring things up. One morning, very early, she went to the owners with, evidently, a major gripe about me. The owner's wife came storming down and chewed me out. I never quite understood what she was so upset about, but suddenly I was fired! Surprisingly, it didn't bother me. I had worked up to my capacity and had no regrets. I was willing to go elsewhere and find a less stressful job. I thought I might even like a break from the floral industry.

Tom, however, was terribly upset. We both were irritated by the fact that I was never given an explanation of why I had been dismissed. But, since Tom had hopes of eventual ownership, he was upset that his partner had been thrown out! I tried to calm him. He thought deeply about the situation for awhile, then decided, "If you're out, I'm out." He gave his notice.

I will always remember the day we cleaned out his office. The owners had been like parents to Tom. He had started working there when he was about twelve years old as a seed planter. After working his way up to delivery boy, and then going to college, he became the manager. I could see he had made a painful decision and I knew he was hurting. Most of all, I saw how much he loved me.

As weeks of unemployment passed, we searched for new avenues and directions. Tom's desire to own his own store did not pass. We went to several floral shops and greenhouses that were for sale. However, the prices were out of our reach. We weren't sure what to do.

Finally, Tom remembered a floral shop broker he met in college. Tom hadn't been in touch with him for several years, so we weren't even sure if he was still in business. We searched through Tom's college papers until we found the broker's business card. Tom dialed the number. We were in luck! He was still at the same place and was willing to show us some shops in Iowa. Since Tom's sister and family lived in that state, we decided to visit them at the same time.

When we arrived in Iowa, the broker showed us several businesses that were within our reach! One he showed us was in the little town of Oskaloosa. The store was small and dark. It smelled musty inside and, to me, seemed uninviting, but Tom was excited.

"Deb, I know how you feel, but this store has potential!" I could tell his business mind was in full gear. Tom was a very hard worker and I was afraid he might allow his job to consume his life. I didn't want him to become a workaholic. I was feeling pretty good healthwise, but I was now more interested in being a homemaker than a career girl. I was also concerned that I might not be up to the physical demands and pressures of owning our own shop. I knew it would demand a lot of time and effort. At the same time, I didn't want to disappoint Tom after he had stood by me. I reluctantly agreed that we should go for it. How was he to follow his dream if I wouldn't allow him the chance to try? He prayed and I worried.

In November, shortly after our first anniversary, we packed up our belongings and moved to Iowa. We had met the previous owners of the flower shop we were buying. Otherwise, we knew no one in Oskaloosa. I was terribly homesick. But soon we began to meet new people and made friends.

Mom and Grandma surprised us by coming during our shop's first Christmas open house. Their help was wonderful. Although we were very busy, this new venture was exciting and I could see how pleased Tom was, which made me happy. I began to feel better about our decision.

We remodeled the store in January. The dingy green paint was covered with soft yellow. We tore out the smelly, stained, black and red tweed carpet and replaced it with a medium brown. The store now smelled clean and fresh and was coming alive. Day by day our new inventory arrived and I was able to design unique and exotic arrangements. The small gift items also added a special touch. Tom was an excellent manager and I was blessed with the artistic talent to design, so we progressed.

One day when I was at home taking a few hours off from the shop to clean house, the phone rang. I thought it was Tom to tell me he was swamped and needed me to come help at the shop. Instead it was my dad. He was completely plastered.

"What's up?" I asked.

"I'm calling to say good-bye," he slurred.

"Good-bye? Where are you going?"

"I've got a gun to my head and I'm tired of living. I'm ready to die and go to heaven, so I just want to say good-bye."

"Dad, don't be foolish!" I cried. I fought to calm myself. Slowly, I continued; "Dad--please--please--put--the--gun--down." How could I know if he even had a gun in his hand? There were three hundred miles between us. But I didn't want to take any chances. I told him I loved him. I told him he was acting foolishly and that only God had the authority to give and take life.

"But I want to go to heaven," he repeated.

"If you take your own life, that's not where you'll be going," I warned.

He began to cry. "I hate my life."

He continued to insist that he was going to go through with his plan. He refused to tell me where he was, so I could not even get help for him. I was terrified.

"Put the gun away, Dad!" I ordered again, impatiently. "If you are going to be so foolish as to end your life, I don't want to hear it over the phone."

Suddenly there was a click and the dial tone hummed in my ear. Slowly I replaced the receiver. Where was Dad? Was he still alive? Was he bleeding to death right this minute? I had no way of knowing and no way to help.

Days went by with no word about Dad. Finally Mom called that weekend. She and Dad were no longer living together and were in the process of a bitter divorce. I hated to ask her about Dad, but I had to know. When I asked, there was a change in her voice.

"That _______ _______ came over just last night and threatened to kill me, your youngest brother, and himself with his gun." She was terribly shaken. As difficult as it was for me to accept, their marriage was coming to an end.

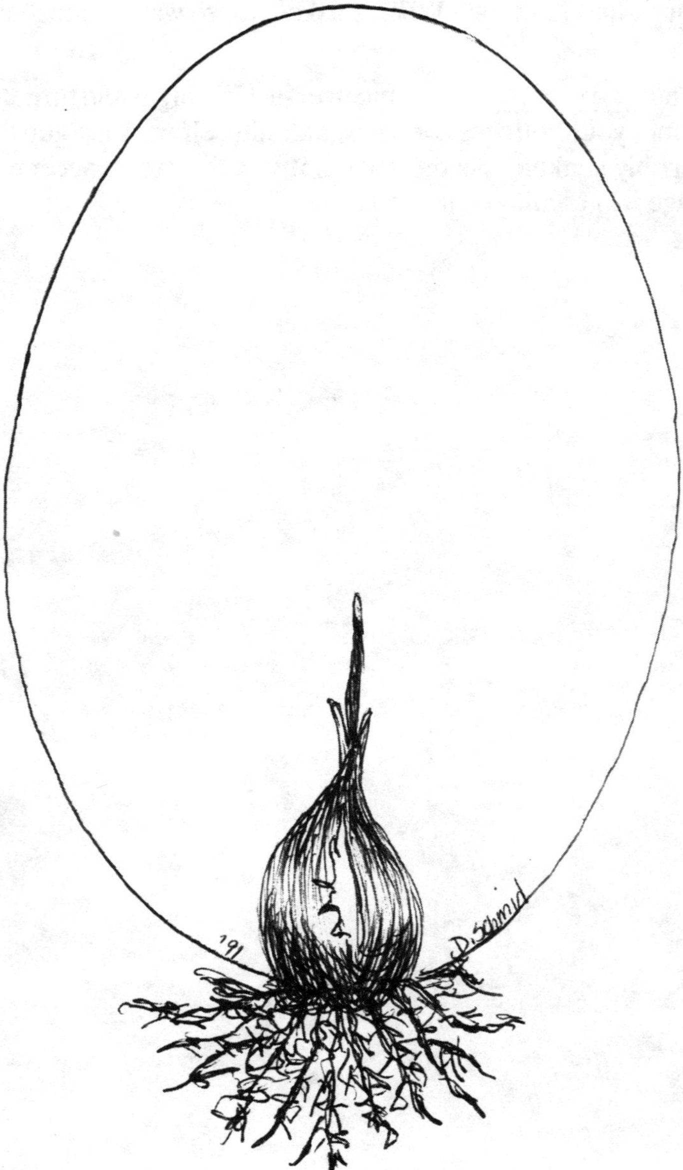
'91
D. Schmid

VIII

New Life

Visions of pink and blue danced in my head. I had been given the hope I needed to start dreaming of diapers and bassinets. At my last physical, the heart doctors told me about some new medical procedures developed to help high risk patients like me tolerate pregnancy more easily. The doctors even knew of several women with heart conditions who had successfully given birth. It required complete bed rest after the first few months and being on oxygen, but there was hope! In spite of my go-around with the priest before we were married, I wanted so badly to give Tom a child and to be a mommy. I was willing to take whatever risk was necessary. My initial reaction was to start looking at wallpaper for our spare bedroom.

Tom was not so sure we should rush into anything. He was worried about my health. He was also concerned about getting our new business established before we took on more responsibilities. He agreed to papering the spare room, but he thought the print should be neutral enough to be appropriate for a guest or sewing room as well as a nursery.

When I told Karen, our new employee, that I was planning to paper the bedroom, she expressed an interest in learning how to hang wallpaper, so I invited her to come help. Karen and I wallpapered while Tom did the shop's book work downstairs. I had learned from conversations at the shop that she was a religious person and seemed to know a lot about the Bible--something I had always been curious about. Many times when I was growing up I tried reading the Bible I had received in Sunday school when I was seven. It seemed I was always searching for something, but was unable to put my finger on it. I thought the Bible might have some answers for me, but I always started reading at the beginning and never got past Genesis. There was a question to which I desperately needed an answer. I had been wondering about it for years. I was not sure how to ask it, but in all my anxiety, it just popped out!

"Karen, is it true that a person has to be baptized to go to heaven?" Many of my friends had been sprinkled as babies and told me it was necessary in order to be saved from hell. Even the priest who married us addressed the issue during our wedding ceremony. Now I needed a truthful answer.

Karen looked up at me, startled, as I stood on the ladder holding a strip of wallpaper dripping on the carpet. The room was silent for only a minute, but it seemed like forever to me. Then she gently replied, "Yes, it is. The Bible says so."

"Oh," I replied. I waited for her to say more, but she seemed to be done. "Well, I suppose I had better do that one of these days then, hadn't I?" I tried to act nonchalant. I wanted desperately to know more, but I was also frightened. Religious matters made me uncomfortable, probably because I was so ignorant. I had had many close shaves with death; therefore, I felt I needed to know what life and death were all about. But it did not happen that evening. We continued to work, and our conversation soon turned to other subjects.

A few months later, I brought the subject up again. "Karen, I feel like there is a God in heaven, but there is a gap between me and Him. Maybe if I got baptized and became a Christian, that gap would close and I would become closer to Him. What do you think?"

She looked at me oddly and suggested that she and her boyfriend come over some evening for a Bible study. I was nervous, but excited. Tom decided to join us. He already considered himself a good Christian, having been raised in the Roman Catholic Church, but he wanted to listen and share ideas.

While Karen and her boyfriend, Merle, were reading Romans 3:23, *"for all have sinned and fall short of the glory of God,"* I clearly understood that "all" included me too. As I continued listening I felt very guilty. I vividly remembered several times when I had fallen for Satan's schemes. I am only human. They taught me John 3:16. *"For God so loved the world that he gave his one and only Son that whoever believes in him shall not parish but have eternal life."* I learned that Jesus died for me and my sins so I could be forgiven and have the hope of eternal life in heaven someday. I realized that He paid an awfully high price for me and I believed in Him immediately.

"What do I do now?" I asked. I desperately wanted to know how to get rid of this terrible load of sin and guilt that was convicting me. Karen explained that since the death and resurrection of Christ, we no longer live under the old law or Old Testament, but under the new law or New Testament. All those years I had been searching for something in my Bible but never read far enough.

We were shown from the Bible that by the grace of God (Ephesians 2:9-10), we can be saved through faith. We learned that faith is a general term used for belief and obedience. We saw in scripture, more than once, the importance of obedience to God (Romans 2:13*). The words of Jesus warned us that without obedience, we shall not see the kingdom of God (Matthew 7:21*). We learned in Acts 17:30* that obedience included repentance and because Jesus humbled Himself unto death, for us, God required us to confess, "Jesus is Lord" (Romans 10:9*). God's salvation required one more step which Jesus commanded, in Matthew 28:18-20* and Mark 16:16*, and His Spirit led apostles taught. We must be baptized (immersed) for the forgiveness of our sins and to receive the gift of the Holy Spirit (Acts 2:38*).

By the end of the evening, I realized I could not go on living as I had. I was afraid to die. Now I knew I was a sinner, bound for hell. I wanted to obey God. I wanted to repent and be immersed into Christ and start a new life, but Tom was confused and upset! What Karen and Merle were showing us in the Bible was not what Tom had been taught growing up. At first Tom became quite defensive because he had been sprinkled as a baby, yet now we learned there was nothing in the New Testament about water sprinkling for salvation. The scriptures spoke about people of reasoning age being immersed--going down into the water and coming up out of the water (Acts 8:38* and Matthew 3:16*). Karen and Merle showed us that the original Greek word for baptize was "baptizo" which meant to dip, immerse, plunge or submerge into water. We were shocked to see how God's Word had been ignored and twisted over the years. For the first time in our lives we understood the simple truth of the Gospel of Christ.

After several questions and hours of intense study, Tom admitted that he had never obeyed God's instructions for salvation and he too, became frightened for his soul. He realized that being a good, moral, even religious person was not enough. Now that Tom's eyes were opened, his stubborn pride broke and he knew that as an innocent baby in his mothers' arms, he was unable to understand sin or God. Tom concluded from biblical facts that his sprinkling had been invalid because he was not capable of repenting of his sins, confessing Jesus as Lord, or willingly obey and give his life to God. In fact, we discovered that the sinless purity of children is what God wanted us to become like (see Mark 10:15*).

That evening Tom and I both decided to leave the ways and teachings of the world and be obedient to God--our Creator and Heavenly Father. About 10:30 that night we all went to the church building. The minister and several Christians met us there to witness our Christian birth, as Tom and I were immersed into Christ for the forgiveness of our sins. Because of our obedience to God, we received the promised gift of the Holy Spirit (Acts 2:38*).

What joy we felt, knowing our sins had been blotted out and God remembered them no more! His generous love had given us the miracle of new hope and a new life--life that lasts forever.*

It's a funny thing about the new life in Christ. Everything is new and beautiful like spring, yet, everything is still old. I still got up at the same time, saw the same face in the mirror as I prepared to go to the same job. I looked across the table at the same husband as we ate our usual breakfast. I was the same me with the same health problems and personality quirks, only now I was under new management. I belonged to God.

I barely knew my new Manager and had so much to learn. He was a good Teacher, but I was not always the most willing pupil.

However, my stubbornness was no match for His determination. He knew me even better than I knew myself. He knew just what I needed. Best of all, He loved me. Whatever life brought, He was there beside me, guiding and comforting me along the way. The question was, would I recognize His guidance and love?

* If you are interested in a detailed Bible study, similar to the one we had with Karen and Merle, please refer to the Appendix of this book.

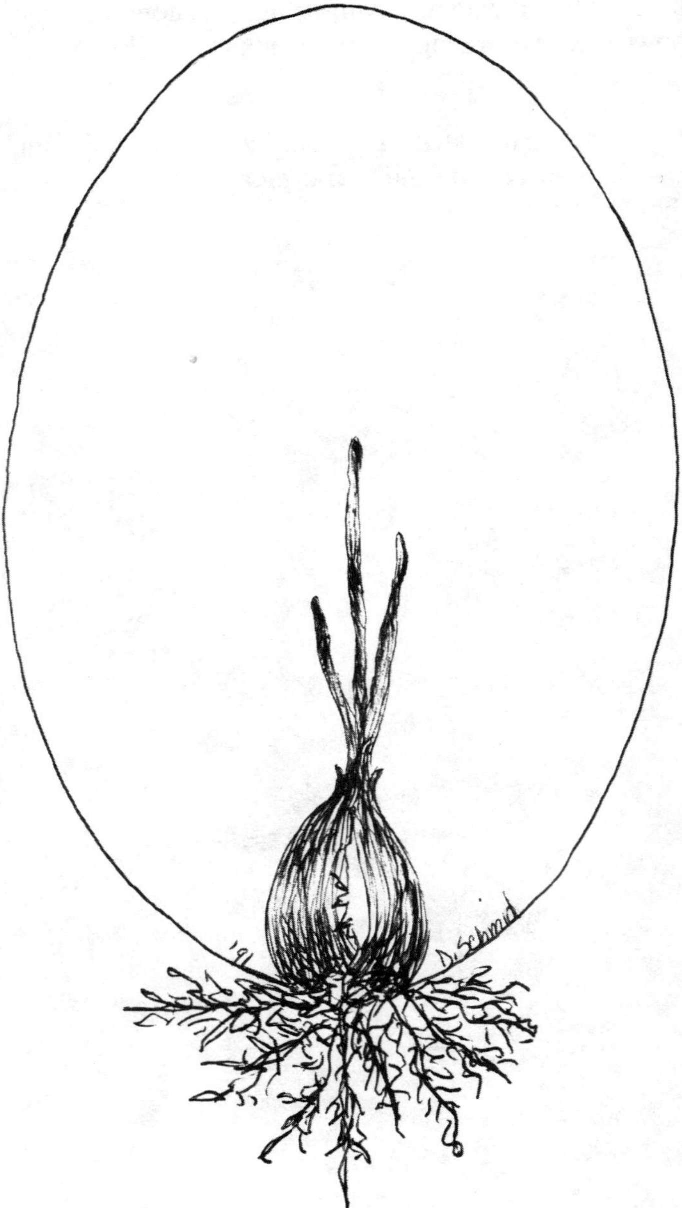

IX

Spring Storms

I heard the tinkle of the bell as the shop door opened and I turned to see who my next customer would be. As the middle-aged woman approached me, sadness hung around her like a cloud. She ordered her flowers, explaining that they were for the grave of her daughter who had recently died from cancer of the uterus. The daughter was only in her thirties. While the woman spoke, my insides froze. My hands shook as I wrapped the flowers. She left on her sad errand, but I could not forget about her daughter.

Even as a teenager I had trouble with my monthly period. Sometimes I vomited or even blacked out from pain. Lately it had been getting worse. During my period I could not even lean against the work table at the shop without getting dizzy and breaking into a sweat. Being on my feet for nine or more hours a day was extremely uncomfortable. Sometimes I felt like a hot knife was ripping into my abdomen and I wanted only to curl up in a ball. My period was also accompanied by migraine headaches for which medicine seemed to do nothing. One week out of four, I was miserable.

Now I was scared. I immediately made an appointment to see my doctor the very next week. I insisted that he figure out what my problem was. He said he suspected endometriosis (the presence of cells lining the uterus, in unusual places such as the bladder or intestinal walls). He referred me to a specialist.

The gynecologist also suspected endometriosis and explained

that surgery would be necessary. Because of my heart condition, he wanted me to go to the University Hospital in Iowa City which was better equipped to handle cases like mine.

Before scheduling surgery, I was examined again in Iowa City. The specialist, Dr. Pitkins, explained the laparotomy he would perform. It was a "simple procedure" in which a small, lighted instrument would be inserted through a small incision in the abdomen in order to look around. He suspected that I also had a cyst on my ovary, as well as the endometriosis, but said he could easily remove it at the same time.

We set the date and I was terrified. Although I was hospitalized many times, I had never been through a major surgery. The procedure may be simple to the doctor, but to me it was a big deal. I called my original heart doctor in Illinois for comfort. He assured me that I was in good hands. I nervously waited through the weeks before the surgery. Spiritually I felt secure, but physically I didn't want to die.

Finally the day arrived. Since I was a high-risk patient, the doctors wanted me to come in several days early for observation and tests. That first night, they released me for a few hours to go on a date with Tom. We went out to eat and then bowling. I had fun, but the whole time I wondered if it would be our last date. The next day was filled with doctors, nurses, visitors, and fear. Dr. Cole, my heart doctor in Illinois, telephoned to tell me that he was thinking of me and to reassure me again. The minister and his wife from the church in Iowa City came to visit me. They were part of my new Christian family. They didn't even know me, yet they cared and loved me enough to come pray with me. In the late afternoon, shortly after Mom arrived, Dr. Epley -- the doctor who would be assisting Dr. Pitkins through my surgery -- came into my room. She kindly explained everything once again and told me to sign on the dotted line. She then asked me if I had any questions. I looked her in the eye and asked, "Can I put my shoes on and go home instead?"

With a surprised look, she answered, "Well, if you want to!"

I burst out laughing. "Just kidding," I assured her. I was making light of the issue to cover up my fears. She chuckled and reminded me that she would see me in the morning. I liked her. There was something special about her that made me feel more comfortable and confident about what lay ahead.

By this time, I was getting hungry. I hoped dinner was coming soon. Instead, another doctor came in with a wheelchair. He informed me that before I could eat, they had orders to insert a tube in my arm. That didn't sound too bad. I figured I would be able to eat in a few minutes. As he started to wheel me from my room, a bouquet of fresh flowers arrived from Tom's brother and his wife. It really brightened my day.

I lay on the table in the cool room, while bright lights glared all around me. Tears flooded my eyes and rolled down my cheeks as the doctors inserted the tube into my arm. I hadn't realized that the tube was to be forced up the vein in my arm and into my chest until it was close to my heart. The tube squeaked as it squeezed through my vein. The sound made me sick to my stomach. I felt weak and tired. The more I thought about it, the sicker I felt. Then suddenly I realized I was not bearing this alone. I started to pray silently and a feeling of peace came over me as the doctors finished the procedure. They told me they would insert another tube in my neck the next morning. I was grateful that I did not have to go through it again right away! Now I understood why they did not allow me to eat first. Then I was moved to a different room on the cardiac floor and served dinner.

My arm throbbed as I visited with Tom and my mom. In no time, visiting hours were over and I was alone. I tried to relax. I was just about ready to doze off when a nurse came in to give me my first Heparin shot. (Heparin is a blood thinner given to reduce the chance of blood clots after surgery.) When I offered her my arm, I was shocked to learn that the shots are given in the stomach! Ouch! That's what I get for signing on the little dotted line!

Shortly afterward, I received several other goodies, such as an enema and a douche. Those nurses were bound and determined to clean me out one way or another. I was so drained by 10:30 P.M. that I was sure I'd drift right off to sleep. Instead, I tossed, turned, prayed, and listened to the shuffling of the nurses almost all night long.

My arm kept throbbing and I couldn't help wondering if I would live through all of this. The doctors told me it was going to be a close one. The last time I looked at the clock, it was 4:00 A.M.

At 5:00 A.M. on the day of the surgery, the nurse came in to give me a shot and some pills to help me relax. It was still dark outside, but Tom and my mom were there to see me off to surgery. I vaguely remember the "good-byes" and "I love yous," but I was pretty far out of it by that time. I hoped and prayed I would return to see them again before long.

As the hours passed, Tom worked on the books from the shop and Mom stitched. Finally I was wheeled into the Intensive Care Unit (ICU). I remember them coming to my bedside later that day, but when I tried to talk to them, they could not understand me. What was wrong with my speech? Apparently the anesthetic had not worn off completely. In time my speech returned, but it was a frightening experience. Tom lifted my sheet so I could see the large gauze bandage on my stomach. I understood that the surgery was over and I cried. I made it! I was alive!

The next day Dr. Epley came to my bedside in ICU. She removed the gauze bandage on my abdomen, took my hand, smiled, and told me I was doing very well. I was still groggy from the medicine I was on, but I tried to listen. She explained that I had the worst type of endometriosis. It had not only destroyed all my female organs, but had spread to my bladder, intestines, and one kidney. The doctors burned it off to keep it from spreading further. It had turned funny colors as well, which meant it was pre-cancerous. She squeezed my hand tightly as she told me that my ovaries were the size of grapefruits and it had been necessary to do a complete hysterectomy.

I was only twenty-three years old! I had only just been given hope of motherhood a short time before. I had been looking forward to starting a family!

"Deb, I'm sorry," the doctor went on, "but we didn't have any other choice." She smiled and left. I was too groggy to think about it then. I was still elated to be alive. I drifted back to sleep to the sounds of beeping machines, shuffling feet, rattling bottles, and the hum of my oxygen mask.

After a few days, Tom and my mom returned to work and I was alone during the day. I was healing incredibly well and needed only a regular aspirin or two for pain.

Now that my head was clear, I needed to talk to Dr. Epley again. "Is it true that I had a hysterectomy?" I asked. Once again she explained the surgery to me. She assured me that, even before the hysterectomy, I would not have been able to conceive since the endometriosis had destroyed my female organs. I listened, composed, until she finished and left the room. Then the reality of my situation hit me and I cried uncontrollably. All hope of ever having a child was gone. I was completely barren. I felt angry with God. Why did He allow this to happen to me? I thought He was my friend. I mistakenly thought Christianity was a cure for my problems, but now I felt like I had more! Was this Lord of mine, who had saved my soul only a few weeks earlier, really deserting me? Was He going to break His promise of His love for me, like others had? Suddenly my lack of understanding allowed my trust in Him to crush, and I stared, unseeing, out the window as the tears spilled down my face. The day dragged on forever as I waited for Tom's evening visit. I needed to hear him tell me he loved me anyway--even though I could never give him a child.

By the end of the week, I was gaining strength and had shed my post-op elastic stockings. Hot flashes, similar to menopause, had set in due to hormonal imbalance. I was anxious to get out of the hospital and back home where we could get on with our lives.

Mom returned to help out for a few days after I got home. That first weekend I sat at the kitchen table arranging fresh flowers for two large weddings booked several months earlier. That's the floral business!

After Mom left, Dad came for a few days. I felt like a little girl again being cared for by my parents.

When Karen, our shop employee, came to visit me, she was bubbling with excitement. Her boyfriend had proposed to her! She asked if I would be one of her bridesmaids. I was delighted.

After two months, I returned to work, starting with half days until I was strong enough to handle full days again.

I began calling adoption agencies across the country looking for a child we might adopt. Everywhere I turned, I received negative responses. Some required that a couple be married a minimum of five years before applying. Others only accepted applicants from certain religious groups. Some rejected us because of my heart condition. That always hurt. Because of the rise in abortions, there were many more adoptive parents than there were babies to adopt.

I have always been upset by abortion. Now I was furious! I wrote letters to Washington D.C. expressing my outrage at the murder of so many of our little ones. What was happening to our country that was built on Christian values?

I struggled daily with the reality of my infertility. I felt defeated and depressed. My hormone medicine was out of balance which caused my moods to swing wildly. Not only did I make myself miserable, but Tom also. One moment I was cheerful and bubbly. The next I was in tears. Tom tried to be supportive. He kept assuring me that he loved me, but I still felt overwhelmed by my problem. When he tried to comfort me by saying that he understood, I snapped, "How can you? You're a man!" Sometimes I was downright hateful. I tried to pray and get close to the Lord, but even that didn't seem to help. Why was God doing this to me? Why?

During this time many of my friends were having babies. Some were even upset because the pregnancy was unplanned and inconvenient. I was usually the last to hear about a pregnancy and that hurt, too. People hated to tell me because they knew it was difficult for me to handle and yet, I didn't like being left out either. Every time I received a birth announcement or a baby shower invitation, I cried. Although I was happy for the couple, it took all I had to maintain my composure while shopping for a gift or sitting through a shower. I wondered if I would ever know a child's love.

I felt the only children I would ever have were my parents. Both called me often with problems and complaints but I was glad to be there for them. Although we were living in different states, I absorbed the burden of their unhappiness. I was happy that they were comfortable talking to me, their daughter. After hanging up, I told Tom that my parents were my children. It seemed we had switched roles.

X

Precious Gift

I craned my neck searching for our friends, Merle and Karen, in the church auditorium. It wasn't like them to be late. I mouthed the words of the hymns along with the other Christians but my mind was elsewhere. Karen's first baby was overdue. Ordinarily the pregnancy of a friend was depressing to me, but this was different. Merle and Karen had invited me to be in the delivery room with them for the birth of their baby. Karen understood how left out I felt and was willing to share her experience with me. I was overwhelmed by the offer. I wondered if I would be in the way or if they might resent a third person hanging around at such a precious time, but they assured me I was welcome.

I attended a few of the prenatal classes along with them in order to prepare myself. Now I was waiting for the first signs of labor right along with Karen.

We were all anxious for the baby to come soon. Merle and Karen were hoping to make an out-of-town move in a couple weeks and Merle was going to begin preaching. Karen needed as much time as possible to regain her strength before the move. I was anxious because Valentine's Day was nearing--one of the busiest times at the flower shop. If the baby did not arrive before Tuesday morning, I would be unable to get away for the birth.

When we returned home from church, the phone rang. It was Karen and she was at the hospital! She assured me that it was still early and there was no need to come yet. Not much was happening.

The afternoon dragged. I couldn't sit still or concentrate on anything. I paced the house. Finally, in the late afternoon, I received the call I had been waiting for--"Come!"

As I approached the hospital, I once again felt awkward. Was I interfering in this couple's life? Did I really belong here? Hesitantly, I went in and the nurse directed me to the labor room. Karen was not in hard labor yet, but she looked uncomfortable. The three of us visited for a little while until Karen became sick. Then the intense pains began. Merle and I tried to comfort her. The woman in the next room came in after Karen, and had already delivered. Karen's pain went on and on. The doctor came in repeatedly to check on Karen's progress. Finally Merle and I were instructed to scrub and put on green gowns as Karen was wheeled into the delivery room.

At 10:43 P.M., baby William entered the world. What a miracle! Even though I was burdened by infertility and still didn't understand the Lord's plan for my future, this experience allowed me to feel God's presence like never before. I instantly knew that He had not deserted me, even when I had been upset with Him. That special moment made me realize that He knows exactly how and when to show His perfect love. God had allowed me to witness the wonder that I had so bitterly resigned myself never to see--the birth of a child. I was overwhelmed with joy. God is so good!

The new location
before we prepared it for moving day.

Moving Day — November 10

Emptying out our little store on moving day —
3 years after purchasing it

Moving large shelving across the city square

XI

Wearing Thin

Tom and I sat on a bench in the center of the town square and watched the sign makers hang a new sign on the store front just opposite our flower shop. It read, "Schmid's Flower Village and Gift Box." Our little shop was bursting at the seams and we had decided it was time to move into a bigger store. Saturday, November 10, a steady stream of cars and trucks loaded with boxes made their way from one store to the other. Some of the larger equipment was pushed across the square on dollies. In the midst of it all, we stayed open for business all day at the old shop. Hundreds of helping hands pitched in to help--men, women, and children. Everyone was exhausted as we stood and sat around in the new shop at the end of the day eating pizza and chicken. Monday, November 12, we were open for business at the new location.

Although the expansion was exciting, I was physically exhausted which was affecting my whole outlook. Tom and I had each been putting in an average of sixty to eighty hours a week at the shop, increasing to eighty to one hundred hours at holiday times. Now the bigger store required even more time. We had employees but it was difficult to get good help for a price we could afford. With the hours we were putting in, our marriage was under a terrible strain. We were both worn out and spent very little time together relaxing or discussing anything other than business. The tension had been building up for several months and we were due for a good argument. One afternoon we disagreed about something and, rather than argue in the store in front of customers and employees, Tom ordered me upstairs to his office. One unkind word led to another, then Tom looked at me, straight in the eyes, and said quietly, "Deb, I really don't feel like you are supporting me in this business." I couldn't believe what I was hearing!

"Oh, you don't, huh?" I cried. "Well, I'll show you what 'no support' is all about!" I turned and hurried back down the stairs to the work room in the back of the shop. I tore off my smock, slapped my knife down on the table, and shoved all the orders onto his side of the table. I was shaking as I stormed out the back door, slamming it behind me.

A drizzling rain fell as I walked home, crying and thinking. How could Tom think I didn't support him? Did he think I liked working my fingers to the bone for hours everyday, even when I wasn't feeling well? Why did he think I had been forcing myself for months to keep going, even when my heart acted up and I had to sneak off and lie down for a few minutes? On certain days, I felt so sick, I didn't think I would live to see the sunset. I was working like a slave, and for whom? It was for Tom! It was for his dream! Now he was saying I didn't support him. The nerve!

By the time I reached the house, I was soaking wet. I reached into my pocket for my house key, then realized I had left it in the pocket of my smock at the store! I sat outside in the gazebo while I racked my brain to figure out a way to break in. By the time I got in, I was pretty miserable, inside and out. I knew our marriage was wearing thin and I wasn't sure what to do about it.

Our backyard gazebo, Oskaloosa, Iowa
One of my favorite places to sit and relax.

Our rock garden

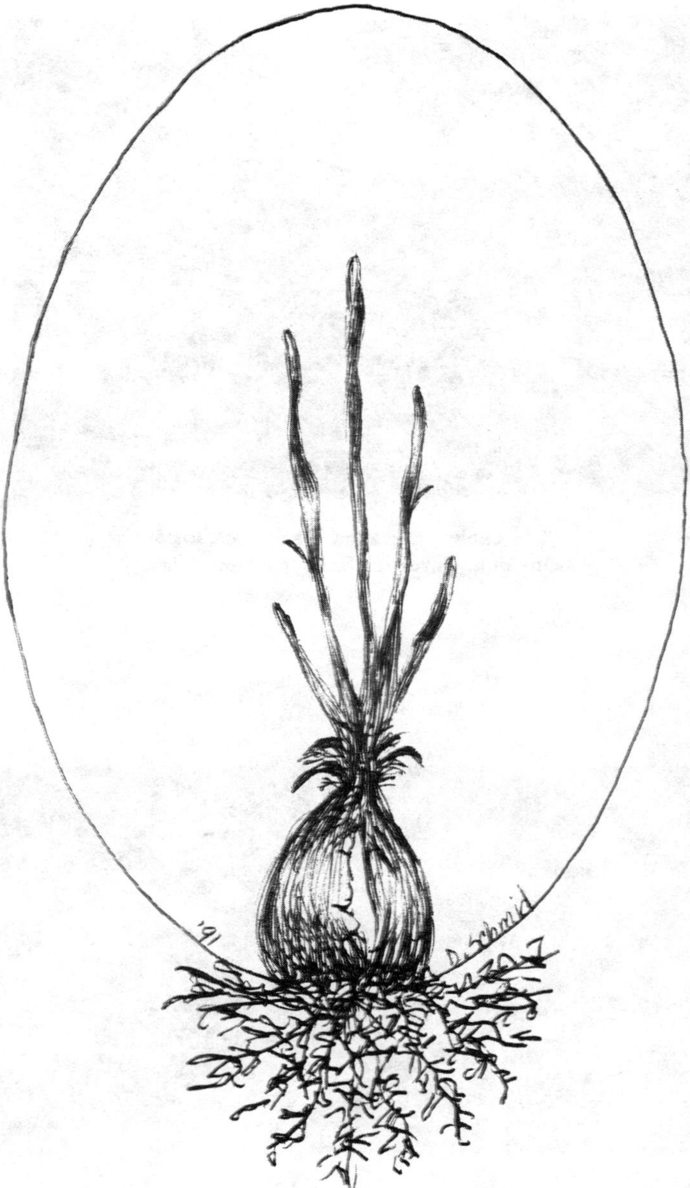
'91
D. Schmid

XII

Unconditional Love

It was Saturday morning and I was working at the shop. Every time the door opened, I turned my head to see if it was Dad. I was expecting him any moment, along with his lady friend whom I was anxious to meet. I was also eager to show him our new shop.

There was another reason I was looking forward to spending some time with Dad. God had been working on my conscience through His Word. He had pointed out that I needed to make things right with everyone in my life. That included working through the grudge I harbored against Dad because of his drinking and the pain it caused our family. In my private reading I came across, *"For if you forgive men when they sin against you, your heavenly Father will also forgive you. But if you do not forgive men their sins, your Father will not forgive your sins"* (Matthew 6:14-15). Yikes! At first I tried to argue with God. "Please," I bargained, "I'll do anything else for you. Anything at all. Just don't ask me to forgive my dad. There's been too much pain. I can't do it." But the Holy Spirit didn't let up.

The more stubborn I became about it, the more I felt myself wither spiritually. Because of my unforgiving spirit, the distance between me and God was growing and I began to become insecure about my own forgiveness. Luckily, God's will is stronger than mine. He didn't let up until I finally gave in. "Okay, Lord. You win! Give me the strength and wisdom to do what I have to do. Help me forgive my dad for all the broken promises and hurts of the past."

That was why I had invited him to come for the weekend. I had great hopes of a warm, father-daughter time together as I envisioned the weekend in my mind. "But, please," I begged him over the phone, "No drinking." He promised. I wanted to trust him, but could I?

About mid-morning, there they were, walking through the shop door. It was so good to see them--my dad and the new woman in his life! After a quick glimpse of the shop, Dad told me they were hungry, as well as curious about the new mall in town. I was busy at the shop and couldn't leave right away, so I suggested some restaurants and encouraged them to look around town. I returned to filling orders with a light heart.

Hours passed. I didn't remember Dad being much of a shopper. Where could they be? As time dragged on, I couldn't help becoming suspicious and anxious. I felt nervous. Finally, about 4:00 P.M., they returned. One glance at my dad and my stomach turned and my face became flushed. His eyes were bloodshot and his speech was slurred as he announced to customers and employees that I was his daughter. I wanted to shut him up and hide him away someplace, but how do you hide a man who is over six feet tall? So much for his promise not to drink. I tried to be pleasant, but the joy of seeing my dad and showing him our new store was gone. The weekend I had envisioned was now ruined by another broken promise. I was crushed.

That evening when the four of us sat in the gazebo in the back yard, I decided I couldn't hold my feelings inside any longer. Barely speaking, I told Dad I'd had it. I could not cope with his drinking. I'd had enough of his lies and broken promises. If he wasn't going to quit drinking or get help, I didn't want to see him again. I told him that I loved him when he was sober, but I couldn't stand him drunk. I refused to let him continue to hurt me. Furthermore, if and when we adopted a child, I didn't want my child to know him as their alcoholic grandfather.

Dad just laughed. "I'm not drunk. You're just over reacting to a few drinks."

In the morning when we woke up, the guest room was empty. There was not even a note of good-bye. So much for my attempt at forgiveness. As soon as he failed to meet my expectations, I was through with him. For all I knew, I would never see my dad again. I had told him that was what I wanted, but God made sure it wouldn't be easy.

I waited, wondered, and prayed. "Lord, I really messed up this time, didn't I?" I kept asking God for wisdom and strength. During the next few weeks, several things were brought to my attention.

I realized that Dad's alcoholism was a disease, not unlike my own heart disease. My heart problems had also caused hardships and financial stress on the family.

I knew that Dad loved me. He had always done everything in his power to help me when I was so terribly sick as a little girl. And he never hurt me when he was sober.

Dad needed my encouragement. He needed someone to love him unconditionally. The Lord wanted me to let go of my own hurts and love my dad in the same way God loves me--without condition or reservation.

Finally, one day my dad called me. He wanted to tell me that he had decided to stop drinking. I'm ashamed to say that I didn't believe him, even after he repeated himself. Rather than thinking of my dad and his feelings, once again I thought only of myself and the hurt of a lifetime of broken promises. I remembered previous attempts to quit drinking as I was growing up. Sometimes Dad had gone several weeks or months without a drink, but always, just when I began to be hopeful that we would be a real family again, he fell back to his old ways. "Dad," I said, "if this is another lie, I don't want to hear it."

Over the next few days and weeks, the Lord continued to show me that I had thrown Dad out of my life at a time when he needed me the most. I became determined to be there for him--unconditionally. This time I wasn't going to let the distance between us stop me from helping him give up drinking if he wanted to try. I prayed constantly that God would give him the strength he needed to help him overcome alcohol. I sent cards and letters of encouragement. I called. I asked others to pray. Months passed and he was doing fantastic! Hope that had almost died inside me began to emerge again. My dad just might make it this time! But even if he stumbled and fell, I would still be there for him--just as my Heavenly Father was for me.

Pretty windows

Silly mannequin in the window.
Merry Christmas!

The first Christmas season in our new store.

XIII

Unconditional Surrender

Over and over I ran into dead ends in my search for a child to adopt. I found a few agencies who would put our name on their waiting list, but all they could promise was a long wait. Everywhere I turned, I felt like I was banging my head against a wall. I guess that was what it took for God to finally get my attention.

As my search dragged on, my heart ached. Why was God putting me through this trial? It was more than I could bear. Why, God? Why? I concluded that I was being punished for the indiscretion of my youth. If only I had saved myself until after I was married, I figured, I would not be childless now. I thought I was paying the price of my sin.

Through God's people, He showed me that is not His way. He had forgiven and forgotten my past and I needed to, as well. Praise God that we are released from the bonds of the past! We live a new life!

But I was still without a baby. All my friends had babies--some even two or three. They complained about the diapers and the discipline. How I longed for their burdens! People told me, "Deb, don't worry about it. Having a child isn't everything!" Those words stung rather than comforted me.

By that Christmas, the emotional pain of infertility was extremely intense and the childless blues had reached their peak. No matter what I did to try to cheer myself up, I just could not get enthused about the beautiful holiday season. Even though Flower

Village danced like a child's wonderland, the decorations at home were kept to a bare minimum. Anything that reminded me of children remained packed away. I wanted to spare myself any extra pain.

How long it took me to get the message! As time passed, I grew spiritually until I discovered the key to this trial. God was not "doing this to me." God was there loving me and caring for me through it all. Satan was the one pulling me down. God was just waiting for me to forgive myself and then surrender my will to His. As long as I had God, I had everything. He was in control of the whole situation. I needed to trust Him. God had an answer to my problem, and it would be a perfect one. I had a deep desire to be a mommy, but if God had something else in mind for me, that was okay, too. I was finally ready to accept it. I let go of my hurt and jumped into His comforting arms.

Spring was coming--my season. I was busy designing spring bouquets for the store. New life would soon be appearing out of doors. April 1, was my day off. I went out for breakfast with a friend and returned home to find a package inside the screen door. A "Flower Village" envelope was attached. I knew immediately it was from Tom. I walked into the kitchen and tore open the box. Inside was a mug that read, "No Mom is half as good as you!" I stared. "What? This can't be!" I read the card. "Congratulations on your new arrival! Call me."

I rushed to the phone. I could hardly see the numbers as I fumbled with the dial.

"This isn't a joke, is it?" I accused when Tom answered. I could tell by his voice that he was also excited. He had just received a phone call from the social worker at the adoption agency, but he refused to give me any details about the baby over the phone. He promised to come home for lunch and talk to me in person.

After I hung up, I tried to pull myself together and tidy up the house. Dirty dishes and laundry both needed attention, but instead, I went to the babies "nursery" and cried. I couldn't believe it was true. I thanked God over and over for entrusting us with a child. I wanted to run right out and get our little bundle of joy.

When Tom came home around noon, he filled in all the details about the baby. We hugged each other excitedly and then made phone calls to our families and close friends. That night at prayer meeting we made the big announcement. I felt like I was dreaming. Was this really true? The next day we made arrangements for our out-of-town trip to pick up the baby. We also prepared the nursery and packed our bags. We were so anxious to meet our child.

We had reservations to catch a flight in the wee hours of the morning on Wednesday. Then Tuesday afternoon we received word from Des Moines that our adoption home studies were inadequate. They were outdated by one month. (These are studies of a couple and their home by a local adoption agency when they apply for a baby.) The state case worker insisted we could not go anywhere until everything was brought up to date and reapproved. That could take weeks! I was an absolute wreck. After working like mad to get things ready at home and at the store, both of us were exhausted. I crumpled into tears.

We called the agency which had done our original study, hoping they could help us out. It was closing time and the agency told us our social worker was no longer employed there. We were going to have to deal with a man we had never met. What a blessing to find him kind and understanding! He told us to come down immediately and he would see what he could do. He interviewed us and assured us that he would speed the paperwork through as quickly as possible.

We left, as scheduled, Wednesday morning, after one and a half hours of sleep. We hoped and prayed that the papers would be completed while we were gone. However, until we received the okay from Des Moines, we were warned that we must stay completely away from the child we were planning to adopt. If not, we would lose all chance of ever adopting a child.

I was scared. We tried to keep ourselves occupied by resting and sightseeing. And we prayed. We trusted God to work things out in His way. We decided that if this was really the child God had prepared for us, everything would work out. If not, then we would go home empty-handed. It was up to Him to work it out according to His plan. We prayed for God's will to be done, not ours.

One week later we returned to Iowa. The air was full of spring as the soft rain watered the tender new grass. Flowers poked up everywhere from beneath the old fall leaves. As we drove into the driveway, we noticed that not only were the trees in bud, but the branches were also covered with big pink balloons. A large sign above the garage door read, "WELCOME HOME--MOMMY, DADDY, AND KYLEA!" (Kilee) We were overwhelmed with joy as we carried our new baby girl into the house and up to her room. What a blessing! The Lord had answered our prayers. The paperwork went through as smooth as silk and the adoption ceremony was beautiful. We waited so long for a child and the moment we saw her, those intense feelings of pain and discouragement, suddenly melted away. Happiness blossomed within our hearts and the reality of parenthood hit hard the first time we heard her cry, and wiped away the tears. She was, indeed, a beautiful little girl, created by God especially for us. God's way is right and wonderful, and it was so good to be a part of it.

The Lord Answered My Prayers

Welcome Home!

I love you sweetheart!

Front outside entry to our store
Springtime

XIV

A Door Closes

Tom was putting in even more hours at the shop. The designer whom I had trained so diligently to take my place, quit. He was now working for our competition across the square. It was not the first time this had happened. We had a hard time keeping employees. By the time we trained them to be efficient in their jobs, they left. Girls often got married and either moved away or had a baby. Other employees simply couldn't handle the pressures of work in a flower shop. But most often, we lost our help due to the wages. We were not able to pay big salaries. We tried to give small raises and bonuses, but there were so many problems in the way. Several merchants from the square had moved into the new mall, leaving the city square half empty. Others went out of business. A local greenhouse put in a floral shop, which meant more competition. The Iowa economy was in a slump and, although business was up at our new location, so was our overhead. To top it all off, our building badly needed repairs. The roof of our building was leaking and windows on the third floor had fallen out. It seemed like Tom and I seldom took any money home. It was a struggle at times to pay the bills and keep food on the table.

People thought we were lucky because we owned our own business, but it seemed like our dream was turning into a nightmare. There was no money for repairs, no money for raises, no money for us! Tom kept insisting that things would get better, but I was getting tired of that line. The question was, "When?" I could now understand why my previous employers did some of the things that used to upset me. It was a matter of survival.

I thoroughly enjoyed being a housewife and mommy, but I knew my absence from the shop added to Tom's burden. I continued to help him with the business as much as possible, doing weddings, silk arrangements, or other special orders at home at the kitchen table. That way I didn't have to leave Kylea with a sitter. When I went to set up the weddings, I took her along with me.

When Tom was in a real pinch, he called me to come in. That was not always easy. Either the baby was napping or I had trouble finding a sitter. When Tom snapped at me, I felt guilty. It wasn't my fault we couldn't keep our employees, however I felt responsible for many of the shop's problems because I was no longer there.

But motherhood came first. I did not have the physical capacity to work and be a mother both. Besides, after our long wait for a baby, I wanted to be home to take care of her. Both of us were tired, but Tom was just about at the end of his strength. By now he was missing most of the evening assemblies at church. I made a special effort to take Kylea and go anyway, but I felt like a single parent. Tom lost more and more weight. He was deathly pale and his height made his appearance even more alarming. Our love life was the pits. One of us was always too tired or sick. Many times when I got up during the night with Kylea, I sat next to Tom and put my hand on his chest to make sure he was still breathing!

During the first six years of our marriage, we seldom argued. Now we fought weekly. It seemed to me that Tom had become a workaholic. He ate, drank, and slept Flower Village. I knew he was doing his best, but it was not working. He was doing things similar to what my Dad had done when I was a little girl. He made promises, but work kept him from fulfilling them. At least my dad was drunk when he broke his promises. Tom was sober and I was hurt.

At night when we shared a snack of popcorn, our conversations were shallow. I began to see my parents' marriage reflected in my own. I tried to talk to Tom about the problem, but he insisted I was imagining things. I knew something had to be done. Satan was trying to destroy our marriage. I needed the Lord's help. I prayed and tried to be patient.

I considered a separation, but I knew the Lord wanted us to stay together and work things out. I also wanted Kylea to have a daddy. Tom accused me of being unsubmissive to him, and I was! The independence of my childhood had kicked in to fill the gap of Tom's absence. I felt like I could handle anything that came my way. In church when the preacher spoke about husbands and wives, I looked at the floor. Submitting to Tom was going against my will, but I knew I was guilty of disobeying God. When I read my Bible, God's quiet words jumped out at me. The Lord was trying to talk to me. He wanted me to live by the Spirit and not by the flesh, but I wasn't listening. Instead, I was being rebellious. No wonder I was miserable.

I found in myself a mirror image of my mom. The more irritated I was with my husband and our marriage, the more moody I became. I was rude to Tom and put on a facade that said, "Hey, I don't care. I can handle this." I really did care very much, and was a wreck inside.

Through it all, I was very careful that we never fought in front of Kylea. I didn't want her to live in fear as I had when my parents fought.

In February we were scheduled for a family photo. The night before our appointment we had another fight and went to bed in silence. The next morning Tom called me from work to tell me that he still loved me. I could not respond. I had been crying all morning. I knew Tom was hurting, too.

That night the last thing we wanted to do was to go to the photographer's, but we went. Tom and I tried to smile and look happy. Kylea shone, as always.

That night I could not sleep. I kept looking at Tom. He looked so pitiful. "What's happening to us?" I wondered. "Our life is the absolute pits."

A few days later, after we both had a chance to cool down and think things over, we had a long talk. We talked about our feelings and about us. We both still cared deeply for each other. It seemed like the money problems were the core of our whole evil mess.

Not only was it causing problems between us, but it also caused stress with employees at work. We had been praying about our financial situation for years and yet it never seemed to improve for any length of time. We wondered if perhaps the Lord wanted us to be doing something else or be living somewhere else. As much as we hated to, we decided it would be best to put the business up for sale. We wanted to draw closer to the Lord and each other and the business was standing in our way.

That summer we waited for a buyer. We had a few prospects, but because of the slow economy and the stiff competition, no one wanted to buy. They had no desire to take on all our problems.

In early fall, we traveled around the east coast area looking for a place to relocate if the store sold. When we returned to Iowa, we were still without a buyer. We decided to proceed with "Plan B." We would simply close out.

On October 25, our eighth wedding anniversary, we held an employee meeting to tell them of our plan. The going-out-of-business sale would begin the following week. It was a painful decision, but Tom and I felt it was our only answer. We both felt weak and empty.

The black paint was diluted with my tears as I painted the big "Going-Out-of-Business Sale" signs to fill the front display windows. But I trusted that the Lord would provide new outlets. As I painted, good memories of the business filled my mind and the hard times suddenly seemed much smaller. I thought about how much Tom and I enjoyed our careers as a whole. He was a great manager and designing came easily to me. I could not imagine our lives without Flower Village. It was so much a part of us. Neither one of us had ever done any other type of work. The thought of change scared me.

I worked at the store the first week of the sale. We were very busy. Customers just could not understand why we wanted to give up our business. Many complimented us on our good work and friendliness. Others tried to talk us into staying. Over and over we heard, "We will really miss you kids." I began to have second thoughts about our decision. I prayed about it desperately and constantly. I knew that the Lord needed to be first in our lives, but the store seemed to be in the way. Or was it? I was confused and needed guidance. If He wanted us to stay in Oskaloosa and work things out, then we needed more business to allow us to hire the help we needed. If it wasn't God's will, then I prayed for Him to show us in a crystal clear way what direction He wanted us to go. We only had one offer to buy the building--for less than half of what we paid for it. I asked for patience and wisdom as I waited for the Lord's answer.

"The sky was filled with thick smoke"
November 6

"Tom! Get up! Flower Village is on fire!"

One Sunday morning in November — "It's still burning."

November 10, four years after moving day.

What a mess! Where do we begin?

XV

Simmering Potpourri

I woke in a cold sweat. It was about 3:00 A.M., Sunday, November 6. In my dream there was a fire in the upstairs hallway and we were unable to get to Kylea! I was shaking as I jumped out of bed and walked through the darkened house looking for flames. Everything seemed okay. The smoke alarm was not buzzing. There was no smell of smoke. I returned to bed and tried to go back to sleep.

When I finally dozed off again, I was startled awake by the ringing of the telephone. I jumped up again to answer it. It was 6:00 A.M.

The voice that answered was familiar. It was a previous employee who lived in an apartment next to our store. We had not heard from him since he quit several months before. He seemed distressed. "Flower Village is on fire." He told me that he had barely gotten out of his apartment alive. Both of his cats were dead. I could not believe my ears. This must be another bad dream.

"Tom!" I called. "Get up! Flower Village is on fire!" Tom was up and out the door almost before his jeans were zipped. I called the fire department to ask if the report was true. They told me that the trucks had gone, but they thought the fire was in the building next to ours. I hoped and prayed that they were right.

I called a friend from church to start a message down the prayer chain so others could be praying, too. Then I went immediately to my knees, asking that God's will be done.

When Tom returned, the stench of smoke hung heavily about him. He cried as he told me what he had seen. Flower Village was indeed burning. The city square was blocked off and the sky was filled with thick smoke. Firefighters poured water into the building as cold, sharp winds fanned the flames into a blaze. Tom was devastated!

By this time the prayer chain had spread the word of the fire and our phone began to ring. Tom left again to go back to the shop. A couple from church arrived to offer their help and support. The husband left to look for Tom. The wife stayed with me. Kylea woke in all the commotion. I made a few calls to our families and then put some rolls in the oven for breakfast. I hardly knew what I was doing.

After eating a little, I decided to go see the fire. The couple from church stayed with Kylea while Tom and I stood in the center of the square watching our business go up in flames. I couldn't help thinking of Matthew 6:19-21:

> Jesus said, *"Do not store up for yourselves treasures on earth, where moth and rust [and fire] destroy, and where thieves break in and steal. But store up for yourselves treasures in heaven, where moth and rust [and fire] do not destroy, and where thieves do not break in and steal. For where your treasure is, there your heart will be also."*

I now had a very vivid understanding of that verse. All our efforts trying to build up a business were slowly turning into charcoal.

We could see flames leaping out of the windows on the upper floors. The crackling could be heard over the roar of the wind. I had trouble breathing as the wind blew smoke and mist into my face. Then, BOOM!, the roof collapsed. Suddenly the sky was visible through the upper windows. Bricks from the third floor wall fell into the alley alongside of the store. A man standing behind us watching the fire said, "Oh, cool!" To him it was just Fourth of July fireworks in November.

Some of our customers came up and hugged us. They offered condolences and tissues as we cried together. A reporter from a television station came up wanting an interview. He wondered if it wasn't ironic that we were going out of business and now the store was burning. He questioned us slyly about the possibility of arson so that we could collect insurance money. We were shocked and insulted. I suppose it must have looked suspicious to many. When the reporter asked, "What are you going to do now?" we answered, "We're going to church." He gave us a strange look. We then turned and walked away. Where else could we turn at a time like this?

As we walked into church, the smell of smoke hung around us. Kylea was tired and cranky. She could sense that Tom and I were upset. When the preacher stood up to speak, he asked us what was happening at the store. "It's still burning," we replied. Silence fell over the auditorium for a few minutes. I could not concentrate on the message. My mind was in shock. As soon as the service was over, we were greeted with hugs and words of comfort. One of the firefighters was a Christian brother. While we were in church, he was fighting the fire.

On our way home, we stopped by the square again. Firefighters from four towns were pouring water on the fire. The building next to ours was no longer burning. Men had entered that building and retrieved the body of someone who had lost his life in the fire. I prayed that the fire had not started in our building. I did not want to be responsible for the loss of a life. Bystanders whispered as we walked by, "There's Tom and Debbie and their baby," or "They're the couple from Flower Village. Look, over there. Oh, what a shame!"

When we got back to the house, Tom's sister and husband were there. They had driven down from Waterloo while we were in church. I tucked Kylea in bed for her nap and we grabbed a quick snack. Then we bundled up and headed back to the store. We were anxious to retrieve anything we could from the building since our insurance did not cover all of our inventory. The fire chief told us to come back in an hour. Before we left for home, he opened the door. Water flowed out like a river! It must had been knee-deep inside the store. Merchandise came floating out with the water. The fire chief snatched up stuffed animals and greeting cards and tossed them back inside. It made a comical sight. As we walked to the van, we saw one of our display cloths lying in the street half a block away.

Later that afternoon we were finally permitted to enter the building for the first time. We walked slowly through the store taking it all in. It was very quiet and peaceful. The water dripped through the ceiling sounding like falling rain. The wind chimes that still hung from the ceiling made quiet music. Some items were in the exact place where we had left them Saturday night, others were floating around in pools of water. The smell of smoke hung everywhere. The plaster on the ceiling and walls was cracked. Everything was soaked. In places the water was halfway to my knee.

As we walked up the steps to our office area, I listened for the sound of our parakeet. All was quiet. The air was thick with smoke and I began to cough. In answer came a loud "Chirp! Chirp!" I rushed to his cage. He was alive and well! In fact, somehow the whole office had remained bone dry! We were able to save our accounts and the cash that had not made it to the bank the night before. What a blessing!

We rushed around, working in semi-darkness because the power was out, trying to load the van with our files, orders, important papers, and the bird. I heard a commotion above us. One of the firefighters was yelling, "Pour more water into the upper window! Hurry!" The fire was burning again. A firefighter came to warn us of the danger.

At 8:00 P.M., the firefighters were still on the job watching for persistent hot spots and pouring water on our building. Kylea and I were down with fevers and sore throats. What a day! All I wanted to do was sleep. I was exhausted both physically and mentally. But sleep was hardly possible. Every time I closed my eyes, I saw fire and smoke. I still heard the crackling and the big boom of the roof falling. Little did I realize that this was the easiest part of the ordeal.

By Monday afternoon, our house was like Grand Central Station. People were calling and stopping by with food, money, and condolences. Tom was in and out all day and the insurance agency and fire department kept our phone lines hot. Kylea and I were both sick and she was very cranky. I sat up for several hours Monday night rocking her and trying to comfort her. She was congested and coughing terribly. I waited anxiously for morning when I could take her to the doctor to get medicine.

Tuesday the fire marshal carefully searched through the debris looking for the cause of the fire. My heart ached as I thought of the person who had lost his life and for his family.

We were not permitted to remove merchandise from our shop until the insurance company came to investigate. They seemed to take forever. The other businesses involved in the fire had already moved to new locations and were setting up for their fire sales. We were still waiting. Our family room looked like the back room of the store. There were tables, files, and boxes from one end to the other. Some of the employees were at our house offering to help. Tom put some to work with the monthly billings. It was critical to have the income. The Flower Village phone lines were now ringing at the house and I was exhausted from running up and down the stairs answering the two phones.

The fire chief called to tell us that if we entered our building, we should do so "quickly and quietly." He said the building was unsound and we should hire someone to tear it down as soon as possible. Tom made tentative arrangements to do so. The only thing holding us back was the insurance settlement.

When the insurance adjuster finally arrived, he reminded us that much of our inventory was not insured. He advised us to have a fire sale. That meant salvaging whatever we could, cleaning it up, and trying to make it saleable. It seemed like the Lord had protected much of our inventory so we would not have such a great loss. I dreaded the work, but considered it a blessing.

God not only saved our merchandise, but also provided hundreds of helping hands. People reached out from all over town to help unload the building, clean things up, and move them to our fire sale location. It was incredible! I was touched to see so many caring people. My dad made a special trip from Illinois to help us. However, we were only able to retrieve things from the ground floor. Somehow, the key to the second floor had gotten lost the night before the fire and was still missing.

By this time word had come to us the fire was caused by an electrical short in a refrigerator cord in the apartment next door. PRAISE THE LORD! I was so thankful that it was not our electrical cord! In the midst of an awful situation, we had a lot to be thankful for.

I never worked so hard in my life as I did the weeks following the fire. I washed well over a hundred loads of wet and smelly stuffed animals, T-shirts, sweat shirts, and linens. In between that and taking care of Kylea, I washed sink loads of pottery, figurines, and glassware. I'm sure the soap companies were pleased that month! I no sooner emptied the living room, when our delivery man backed the van up to the door and unloaded another batch. I was becoming discouraged. I had helpers, but I could not see the end.

Reporters continued calling and, if all this was not enough, the city was putting a tremendous amount of pressure on us to restore the fire-damaged building. It was a historical landmark and a prime building on the city square. They felt all efforts should be made to preserve it. We agreed in theory, but did not have the money for such a project. That was why we were going out of business.

Finally, January 21, we held our Flower Village auction to get rid of everything left over after the fire sale. Whole tables full of leftover merchandise sold for twenty-five or fifty cents. It was difficult to watch. I was so thankful that a couple from church came to spend the day with us. It was hard to hold back the tears as the sale came to an end. After cleaning up, we lowered our sign and locked the door to Schmid's Village and Gift Box for the last time.

One long and dreary winter — Flower Village after the fire

We made it! 10 years together

XVI

Spring Again

What were we to do now? The business was gone and the dreariness of winter filled the skies day after day. Tom had sent out over one hundred resumes but had very few leads. The insurance from the fire was unsettled and the fate of the burned buildings was still undetermined. February was here. Valentine's Day had always been one of our busiest times at the flower shop. We felt lost without our business. We decided to leave town for a few days for a little vacation feeling we needed a break from Oskaloosa and a chance to pull ourselves together.

As Tom unloaded our luggage, he discovered the key to the second story of our burnt building that had been lost since the night before the fire. Apparently it had fallen out of his pocket and slipped down between the seats. During our trip it worked its way onto the floor of the van. We were anxious to go exploring when we returned home.

I like adventure, but even I was nervous about being on the second floor of an unstable building. The ceilings were falling in and the walls were charred. The smell of smoke lingered in the air. We climbed the blackened staircase to peek at the third floor. With the roof gone, the third floor was exposed to the winter elements, so snow and ice had made the stairs even more treacherous. My heart sank and tears filled my eyes as I quickly looked around. Then I scooted back down the steps on my behind. I was anxious to get back to solid ground. We grabbed the candelabra from the second floor on our way down because we knew someone who was interested in buying them.

Tom received a few job offers, none desirable. He wanted a sales representative job, but the offers he received required that he be away from home fifty to eighty percent of the time. That was what we were trying to get away from. We needed time to be a family. Sometimes when I was especially discouraged, I called a Christian friend who was like another mother to me. She continually encouraged me by saying, "Debbie, don't give up now. Keep leaning on the Lord. Things will work out. Just think of how far He has already carried you in these last few months. Lean on Him." That gave me the extra boost to keep going. But, waiting was so hard.

Our lives were heavy with uncertainty and, although the days following the fire were difficult and stressful, soft words of concern and time spent together were welcomed, and offered a refreshing ray of hope to our relationship. With nothing settled, we decided to take advantage of our free time to visit my mom on the West Coast. We seemed to be able to think things through better when we were away from home. On our way to California, we stopped to visit some friends in Arizona. The girl had worked at Flower Village before she married and moved out west. Her family still attended our church in Oskaloosa. When we arrived, the weather was beautiful. Spring was in the air. The birds were making music and the flowers were in bloom. Beautiful mountains loomed in every direction.

After an overnight stay, we proceeded on our way. That evening Tom called our home answering machine from the motel and found a message about a job offer. One of the owners of the business making the offer lived in the town where we were staying. Tom called him and an interview was arranged for the next morning. The offer was for a sales representative job like Tom wanted. The area it covered was small enough that we would be able to spend time together as a family. Not only that, but the area he would serve was in Arizona, where our friends lived! It was exciting to think we could live so close. However, there was one major catch--the pay was straight commission with no benefits. We took it to the Lord in prayer.

We decided to return to our friends' house and check out the town a little more. We looked at homes in the area and came across one that was perfect for us--ranch style with no steps for me to climb and a beautiful view of the mountains from every direction. I was concerned about the altitude since it was higher than I was used to, but the doctors felt that the difference was minimal and I would easily tolerate it. The idea of milder winters was very appealing. But what about finances? We knew that money matters could make even a beautiful day seem gloomy. Tom and I finally decided that since the Lord had carried us this far, He certainly was not going to forget us now. We decided to go out on a limb and hang on to our faith.

Once we had decided, we needed to get busy! Suddenly there was an endless number of things to be done--a home in Oskaloosa to sell, packing to do, a yard sale to prepare for and, worst of all, the good-byes. Our days were completely full.

The fire-damaged building was sold to a couple willing to restore it. We had a big moving sale that seemed almost like a going-away party! Many people showed up, not only to buy but to say good-bye and wish us well. We were touched by everyone's love.

Our last Sunday in church was a day we had dreaded. The only thing comforting me was the thought that this separation was only temporary. As Christians we have the hope of being together again in heaven for eternity.

Then, suddenly, it was time to leave Iowa. The movers finished packing and we were ready to go. While Kylea waited in the car, Tom and I took one last walk around the back yard. I could see the Lord's beautiful handiwork in bloom everywhere. The gazebo and rock garden we had built were now waiting to be enjoyed by a new family. Signs of spring surrounded us. We got into our van, but no one said a word. Our hearts and minds were full of memories while we headed off for a new start. We held hands as we drove off, but we didn't look back. We were together and in God's care. Spring was here again. The days ahead were bound to be beautiful.

'91
D. Schmid

XVII

A Quiet Brook

It was a bright summer morning, just a few months after our move to Arizona. I woke up and looked around the room. As I viewed the familiar surroundings, I felt at home. We were settled in now, but were also looking forward to a trip back to Iowa and Illinois in a few days. Tom's folks were celebrating their fiftieth anniversary and we planned to be there.

As I started to get out of bed, I felt strange. My entire right side, from my neck to my toes, was numb. I had virtually no use of my leg and my arm was very weak. Although it was unusual, I did not panic or get upset. Tom had woken up to find his right hand paralyzed a few weeks before. He apparently slept on it wrong and it healed again in time. I assumed I must have done the same thing.

I hobbled around dragging my leg behind me while I did my morning chores. Tom tried to convince me to call my doctor, but I resisted. I hated to bother him for something so foolish. I finally called, just to please Tom, but my regular doctor was on vacation. I asked the receptionist if she would have someone else return my call. "It's nothing urgent," I assured her. "I think I just slept funny, but I'm not sure." I was in no pain and felt composed.

Tom hesitated to leave me and go to work. He paced around the room. "Maybe I should cancel my appointments today. I don't think I should leave you here alone."

"Oh, don't be silly," I answered. "It's nothing to worry about.

Besides, I'm not alone. Kylea's here with me."

"That's all the more reason I should stay home," he replied.

"Don't worry. I'm fine," I insisted. "You better go before you miss your first appointment."

He gave me a list of customers he planned to see that day, just in case I needed to reach him. After he left, I dressed Kylea and we ate breakfast. I decided not to go to the ladies' Bible study that morning. I knew I couldn't drive in my condition. I called the study leader.

"Hi, Madeline. This is Debbie. How are you this morning?" I asked.

"Fine. How about you?"

"Well, not so good. Something strange has happened to my right side. It's numb. I'm not sure what's wrong with it."

"Did you call your doctor?" she wanted to know.

"Yes, but he's not in. Someone else will return my call this afternoon."

"Afternoon!" she cried. "You can't wait until afternoon. Debbie, I'm concerned about this. Do you think it's something in your water?"

"I don't know, but it could be since Tom had a similar episode. Maybe we should have it checked."

"Well, you call me back after you hear from the doctor, okay? We'll be praying for you. If I can help in any way, just call me."

"Okay, I will. Thanks a lot. I'll talk to you later. And don't worry about me. I'll be fine."

By lunch time, I was feeling very dizzy. It seemed like everything else was going wrong, too. A repair man came to the house and his speech overflowed with foul language. I tried not to let him see how weak I was. I didn't trust him. Kylea acted like a typical, independent toddler, and the doctor still didn't call. The rest of the morning passed in a blur. When I put Kylea down for her nap, I decided to rest, too. My arm was a little better, but my leg still felt like rubber.

The doctor finally called about 2:30 P.M. When I explained my symptoms to him, he said, "Go to the emergency room immediately. I'll meet you there."

I called a friend to baby-sit Kylea and caught Tom just in the nick of time as he was about to leave from his last scheduled appointment.

The doctor in the emergency room did several nerve tests. One of the tests was to tap me with a pin from my right side to the left. When he got to the center, I said, "Ouch!" I had felt nothing to that point.

"Debbie," the doctor said, "I want to admit you for the night."

"I don't think that's necessary." I replied. I was worried about the expense. But after talking it over with Tom, I decided we could probably handle one night.

By Wednesday, I had improved a little, but still felt weak and numb. The doctors kept ordering various tests for me. I was starting to wonder what was going on. Their first diagnosis was that I had a complicated migraine, but they weren't sure.

When the nurses poked needles into the veins of my feet looking for blood clots in my legs, I cried. It hurt so badly. But I'm sure it was nothing compared to the pain that Jesus suffered on the cross when He was crucified. Nails driven straight through His hands and feet had to be painful. He paid a terrible price for you and me. My physical pain took my thoughts back to the mocking and emotional pain of my childhood. Jesus was mocked because of who He was, too! I was only a skinny little kid with a heart condition. Jesus was the Son of God! Rejection hurts!

After the nurses removed the needles from my feet, they bandaged them and put my socks back on. I smiled and said, "Oh, just cover them up and pretend nothing happened." The nurse looked at me strangely and said, "I can take them off if you would like me to." I chuckled and told her I was just teasing. My strange sense of humor helped me tolerate the pain.

Sometimes people treat Jesus the same way. They believe that if they cover their ears and eyes to God's Word, the scars from Jesus' death on the cross will be hidden. People just don't realize the pain and rejection He suffered for us.

After a heart sonagram, X-rays, cat scan, and halter monitor, the doctors ordered an M.R.I. scan. It sounded like a simple procedure and since there was no pain involved, I thought nothing of it. When I arrived at the room where the scan was to be performed, I was asked to lie down.

"Do you have a problem with claustrophobia?" the technician asked.

"No, not to my knowledge," I replied. Then she put a hard mask over my face and started to strap me down. I began to panic. She then rolled me into a long, capsule-like structure. I felt like I was being put into a coffin. I insisted that she let me out. She wheeled me halfway out and told me, "The test will only take about forty-five minutes. Please remain quiet. If you need anything, press this little emergency button, okay?" Only forty-five minutes? That was forever! My hands were sweaty and I fought panic. All I could do to calm myself was to close my eyes and pray. The time passed in slow motion, but the Lord helped me get through it.

I had resigned myself to the fact that we were not going to be able to go on our vacation to Iowa and Illinois. I think it was easier for me to accept than it was for Tom. I was accustomed to missing out on things due to illness, but I felt terribly guilty that he would have to miss his parents' celebration. I tried to convince him to go without me, but he said, "No." He felt a deep need to be with me. Tom's love and concern were comforting in the face of this new trial.

The next day the doctors came into my room to explain the results of the tests. "The M.R.I. scan showed evidence of previous strokes, so we have reason to believe that this episode was also a slight stroke." It was difficult to even think that at twenty-nine years of age, I was the victim of not one, but several, slight strokes. As I thought back, I recalled other times when I felt tingly, but not sick. Those episodes must have been strokes, too. It probably sounds strange that I didn't panic, but when you have had so many ups and downs in health, I guess you learn to accept these as a part of life.

The Lord blessed me through it all. I never lost my memory

or vision, and I regained ninety-eight percent of my damaged right side. Most importantly, I never lost my spirit or my smile. God really loves His children and He showers us with His protection every day.

One afternoon, one of the doctors came to talk to me. She said, "Debbie, you're going to have to calm down and take life a little bit slower."

Calm down? Take it easy? I hated those words. I often felt like a hostage to my own body. I had a tremendous desire to be busy and to live life to its fullest. My philosophy was that life is precious regardless of what this world throws at you. This has helped keep me going through all the pain and upheavals in my life. Calming down and living a bit slower was going to be a challenge for me.

I mentioned to a friend that I thought being calm would be boring. "You don't have to be boring to be calm," she told me kindly. She was right. I felt just as excited sitting beside a quiet brook as I did by a roaring ocean. A quiet, bubbling brook gives a feeling of joy and tranquillity. I just had to turn my back on those roaring waves and concentrate on the brook. I decided I wanted to protect my health for as long as I could. I wanted to be able to spend many happy years with Tom and to watch little Kylea grow.

'91
D.Schmid

XVIII

My Heart Transplant

As the months passed, we all adjusted to our new life. Of course, we had the normal struggles of a major move and career change but, for the most part, things fell into place.

We were now able to spend more time together as a family and I made a renewed commitment to draw near to the Lord. However, stressful situations continued to inject themselves into our lives and it seemed like the more I tried to calm down, the more jittery I felt.

My health weighed heavy on my mind as doctors pressed me to consider the future option of a heart/lung transplant. For months I wrestled with that decision. Tom and I were getting along better, but I knew we needed to continue working on our marriage, especially in the area of honest communication. And I was still haunted by the mystery of my failed relationship with Walley. After eleven years, I had not figured out what went wrong and I felt like that chapter of my life was unfinished. The unresolved issue concerning Walley continued to keep me in bondage, and as a result, I felt like my relationship with Tom was at a dead end.

The worst factor of all was that spiritually, I seemed to be going through an all-time low. When I say "low," I mean rock-bottom low. From the outside, everything looked perfect: a new home, two cars in the garage, a job for Tom, an opportunity for me to be a full-time mommy, a child to love, and, most importantly, I was a Christian. Yet, I was walking around in tears all the time and I didn't know why. Christians are supposed to be joyful, not downcast. We are children of God! So what was wrong with me? I wrestled continually with this dilemma. I tried so hard to do God's will, yet I felt like a failure.

I prayed without ceasing for God's healing hand to be upon me and sometimes I even asked others for advice. Finally, one of my dearest friends wrote: "Debbie, may I suggest that you use that fire and determination of yours to mend your marriage and rest in the Lord." I knew exactly what she was getting at, and I was touched in a special way as I finished reading her letter. An unhappy spirit or marriage is not from God. As soon as I realized the areas of my life that Satan was attacking, that spark ignited and a fire began to burn in me. I was determined that Satan was not going to control me or my marriage any longer.

The next day, I started to feel those spiritual growing pains during my daily Bible study. I discovered a huge missing piece to my puzzle. It was as simple as *"God is love"* (from 1 John 4:16).

Even though I had now been a Christian for several years, I had never come to grips with the true nature of God. Because of what life had taught me, my concept of God was way off. Life had taught me hostility, anger, insecurity, resentment, loneliness, disappointment, worthlessness, ugliness, rejection, fear, inadequacy, impurity, distrust, and devastation.

Before I became a Christian, I used human coping mechanisms to survive pain. My worst enemy was myself and the dreadful wall I had built around myself for so many years--a wall of stubbornness, isolation, toughness, suppressed feelings, distrust, busy-ness, false fronts and, worst of all, the need to be in control of everything around me. My facade was nothing more than a broken heart covered with a smile. My walls were so thick, it was not surprising that I didn't understand who God really is. Every time someone tripped my trigger, I instantly slapped on another layer of whatever ingredient I felt was suitable for the situation. How could I possibly be a light for the Lord when I was isolated behind layers of "protective" walls? When I realized what I was doing, I asked the Lord to forgive me and destroy those walls. As His child, they were unnecessary. I found the Lord was my protector and with His armor, I could handle everything in my life.

The Bible says in Ephesians 6:11, *"Put on the full armor of God so that you can take your stand against the devil's schemes."* It goes on to explain what the armor of God is. In verses 14-17, it says: *"Stand firm then, with the belt of truth buckled around your waist, with the breastplate of righteousness in place and with your feet fitted with the readiness that comes from the gospel of peace. In addition to this, take up the shield of faith, with which you can extinguish all the flaming arrows of the evil one. Take the helmet of salvation and the sword of the Spirit which is the word of God."*

Who needs walls when we can stand in an open field with the Lord and His protection? As I continued to find even more spiritual truths to aid me in my weakness, I became more and more excited.

I memorized one of the most important verses I found. It made a deep impact. In 1 Corinthians 13:4-8a, the Bible describes love:

"Love is patient, love is kind. It does not envy, it does not boast, it is not proud. It is not rude, it is not self seeking, it is not easily angered, it keeps no record of wrongs. Love does not delight in evil but rejoices with the truth. It always protects, always trusts, always hopes, always preserves. Love never fails."

Since God is love, I then replaced "love" with "God."

God is patient, God is kind . . ., God never fails.

When I finished with this simple exercise, I was astonished at what I had learned about the Almighty God. Everything finally came into focus and I could see why I had been at rock bottom. I had made God too small. No one in their right mind would want to trust my little "god." As the days passed and the tears flowed, God's Son shone upon me. The rainbows that followed were beautiful and as peace filled my heart, I began to calm down.

My attention was next directed to my heart transplant. I am not speaking of my physical heart here. In spite of the doctors' recommendations, I had no desire to go through a physical heart/lung transplant. The heart transplant I was interested in was the spiritual one performed by the Almighty God. When I was baptized, I came in contact with the blood of Christ. The Bible says *"Therefore, if anyone is in Christ, he is a new creation; the old has gone and the new has come!"* (2 Corinthians 5:17).

My physical body was the same, but God's Spirit gave me a heart transplant. I had been rejecting my new organ. The infection of my old life had been poisoning my new heart all these years. I had allowed Satan to convince me that what my old life had taught me was true, but it wasn't. Satan is the father of lies (John 8:44).

To God, I am justified, holy and righteous in his sight (Colossians 1:22). God saw me through rose colored glasses, colored by Christ's blood. Because I obeyed Him, the Bible says, the Lord will never leave nor forsake me. All the love, security, acceptance, and assurance I needed were found in Him and no one else.

I'm so ashamed to admit that I made my "god" too small for so long. I expected secular idiosyncrasies and imperfect people to give me what only God could provide. I pictured Him like all the men in my life had been, from my dad clear through my husband. Because of my terrible misconception, Satan had the upper hand for a long time. I finally quit trying to poison that special heart with which the good Lord blessed me. I am so grateful that the Great Physician didn't allow me to continue to reject my new heart, but to completely accept it and let go of the old self. He protected me from a deadly infection and kept me in His care. What a wonderful and patient God we serve! We can live happily ever after when we truly rest in Him.

I no longer possessed that desperate need to control everything in my path nor to be the commander on my battlefield. It was so much easier to submit without all those walls. Now when the devil fired his darts, I knew that, regardless of what Satan or anyone else did or said to me, with the breastplate of faith, I would be protected. I could rest in Him and trust Him for all things. No ammunition that Satan used could destroy Christ, who lived in me. Christ died and overcame every obstacle in my past, present, and future. With Him in me, I had the power to overcome them, too.

XIX

Spring Blossoms In My Life

As I reflect on the seasons of my life, I can see the spring blossoms that have brightened and fragranced my path. The Lord made something beautiful of what might have been weeds and thorns.

My heart condition has always put physical limitations on me, but they have been few compared to others. Despite the fact that I am currently on oxygen fifteen hours per day, I feel blessed that every morning when I wake up, I can get out of bed, take a walk, hug a friend, share a smile and give thanks to God for another day of life. I have much more to be thankful for than not.

The Lord chose when to put me into the world, and when I have completed the work He has prepared for me, it will be time for Him to take me home to be with Him for eternity . I am trusting in His judgement. I know that whatever day it will be--today or fifty years from now--it will be the perfect day. I have entrusted all things to Him. My family, our home, our finances, . . . but, most of all, myself. I know deep inside that He will take care of everything according to His will, not mine.

While I was growing up, my mother was under a great deal of emotional stress. Many times I didn't understand her or her actions and, as a result, I often felt hurt. After outgrowing that awkward stage of adolescence and becoming a wife and mother myself, I realized how giving, caring, and special my mother is. I know in my heart that she did her best under the circumstances, while I was growing up, and I harbor no ill feelings from the past. During the past few years we have become quite close. I often think of her as my "best friend." There is something very special about a mother's love.

Substance abuse is an awful thing to experience. My dad's drinking not only affected himself, but everyone with whom he had contact. As his daughter, I accumulated bitterness and hatred towards him because of it. It wasn't until after I became a Christian that I could forgive my dad. I knew God had forgiven me and, to have the Lord's peace, I needed to forgive others . . . including my dad. I am so thankful he was able to stop drinking several years ago. I am now enjoying the father/daughter relationship I had always dreamed of sharing.

Dating was an awkward experience, but my broken engagement shattered me and my tender young heart beyond repair for many years. I regretted deeply that I had given in to Satan's scheme of premarital sex and, as a result, that was by far the most painful and long-lived trial I have faced. Being a teenager was tough, but God was tougher. I wasn't even a Christian then, but when I look back, I can see God was working in my life and loving me all along.

Interestingly enough, while I was in the process of writing this book, Walley resurfaced in my life. After eleven years, he came to visit me and we talked about what happened when we broke up so long ago. I was able to have my questions answered, return his ring and stereo, and close that chapter of my life. That bitter root has been replaced with forgiveness and friendship. What a relief! Now my marriage can blossom like never before.

Infertility also overwhelmed me. That painful wait for a child seemed endless and unbearable until the moment I held our daughter in my arms. She is such a joy and blessing and I thank God for the privilege of motherhood.

Losing our family business was another traumatic event, but I am thankful we had an opportunity to follow our dream and make it a reality. I do not feel that we failed; instead, I feel we succeeded. It was in that little town in Iowa that I was introduced to Jesus and became His child. I have found so much joy and inner peace since becoming a Christian. I am thankful we lost our business and not our souls.

Although my spiritual heart transplant was difficult and painful, I can say that the Great Physician has healed the wounds and the scars have finally vanished. In times of trouble, I no longer question my Lord. It's not necessary. Every trial has taught me a very important lesson and has brought me closer to the Lord. I feel blessed that He cares about me so deeply. God is powerful and loving and I try to keep Him first and in complete control of my life. He has a special plan for each and every one of us. We need to be patient. Sometimes that's difficult in a society that demands everything NOW!

The Lord has always seen me through my trials and after each one, I come out that much stronger and refined in Him. I know that if I even dared to ask my Lord, "Why?," His answer will be, "I love you Debbie, and it's almost time for spring."

D. Schmid
'91

Acknowledgments

Thanks to my parents for helping me endure my various illnesses and always providing for my physical needs while I was growing up. I love you both very much.

I wish to thank my grandparents, Dr. Cole, Joan and Bernie, and Mrs. Scherer for filling in when my parents were absent. And to my dear friends Kim and "Walley," thanks for all your love, support, and encouragement throughout the years.

Many thanks to all of my former employers for giving me the opportunity to work and learn a trade. I am very grateful that you allowed me the opportunity to earn needed money for many of my goals.

A special thank you goes out to all of you who have helped me in various ways and supported me in writing this book, especially Lois Knutson and Carlene Franklin. God bless both of you for your many hours at the computer. Lois, I also appreciate your willingness to share your creative writing skills in my book. The Lord originally wrote this book before I ever considered it. Anyone's life, with God at the core, will be a literary masterpiece with a happy ending.

To my husband, Tom,

Thanks for the generous amount of love and understanding you so freely give to me. Also, for tolerating my moods and enduring our trials. Only a man with an abundance of patience could be married to me. I appreciate your love.

Tom and I both want to thank Karen and Merle for your friendship and for showing us the biblical truth and helping us to understand the way of Christ.

Thank you, God, for saving our souls.

Last, but not least, I cannot forget God's special little gift to us, our daughter Kylea. Although you are still a little girl, I know you will undoubtedly face some of the same trials and temptations that I did. I only pray that you will be blessed with the strength to make the right choices. I also pray that in your trials, the Lord will bless and strengthen you as he has me. Always remember, I love you and spring is just around the corner!

A Heart-to-Heart Message to My Readers:

I hope you read something in my story that spoke to you in a special way. I pray I was able to encourage you not only to appreciate your life here on earth, but to help you realize that it is only temporary and even when life is hard, the Lord can make it beautiful.

Many people whom I dearly love, have told me that Christianity is based only on what you believe. They say it doesn't matter what you do. Those words make my heart cry. True Christianity is more than believing. It's a commitment to God and His Son, Jesus. It is vitally important that we look at the complete Bible for His guidance and that we respond to the entire will of God, not just to the parts we like or choose. Jesus said, *"Not everyone who says to me, 'Lord, Lord' will enter the kingdom of heaven, but only he who does the will of my Father who is in heaven"* (Matthew 7:21).

If you are not a part of the first century church that Christ built, with God and Christ as the only Head, or, if you have not followed Jesus' divine teachings, then my prayer for you is that you would have the strength, wisdom, and desire to search for and follow the only way to heaven--His way.

In love, and in conjunction with Chapter VIII, New Life, I would like to share with you a simple Bible study from God's Word. Many of the questions have been taken directly from our study with Karen and Merle or from studies I have had with others.

The Bible says, *"for all have sinned and fall short of the glory of God,"* (Romans 3:23). We all need to be saved by the Lord. Trust in Him and not your own insights. *"For we know him who said, 'It is mine to avenge; I will repay' and again, 'The Lord will judge his people.' It is a dreadful thing to fall into the hands of the living God"* (Hebrews 10:30-31).

I want to encourage each and every one of you to give God a real chance to work in your life. If you do so with a sincere heart, I can promise you that you will never be the same again. Don't let Satan pull you down when Christ Jesus is ready and waiting to lift you up and someday take you home.

Jesus carried the weight of the world on His shoulders. Remember, eternity is forever! Let the everlasting "Beauty of Spring" and "New Life" in Christ touch your heart, too!

May God bless and guide you as you study His Holy words.

In Christian love,

Debbie Schmid

Appendix

The Lord's Perfect Plan for Eternal Salvation

Before you begin, I encourage you to pray to God, in Jesus name (John 15:16 and Colossians 3:17), for wisdom and guidance. Don't be afraid to ask Him for an open heart and a clear mind.

I have spent many hours studying the scriptures and the biblical plan of salvation. Several of the Bible references are written out to aid those of you who might not have a Bible. If you do have a Bible, please feel free to use it as you study.

On this _______ day of ___________________, I earnestly searched the scriptures and studied out the Lord's plan of salvation.

____

Your Signature

WHO IS GOD?

God is our heavenly Father and the creator of all things.

"In the beginning God created the heavens and the earth" (Genesis 1:1). *"So God created man in his own image, in the image of God he created him; male and female he created them"* (Genesis 1:27). *"God saw all that he had made, and it was very good"* (Genesis 1:31a).

WHO IS JESUS?

Jesus is the Son of God.

While Jesus was on earth, God called from heaven and said, *"You are my Son, whom I love; with you I am well pleased"* (Mark 1:11b).

WHERE DID JESUS ORIGINATE?

"In the beginning was the Word, and the Word was with God, and the Word was God. The Word became flesh and lived for a while among us," (John 1:1 and 14).

Jesus was the Word who was with God when all things were created. Later on, He became flesh and lived on this earth.

WHY DID JESUS COME TO EARTH?

Jesus came to earth, as God's sacrificial lamb, to take away the sins of the world (John 1:29). He was tempted and tried just as you and I are, only He remained perfect and holy unto death.

"He committed no sin, and no deceit was found in his mouth. When they hurled their insults at him, he did not retaliate; when he suffered, he made no threats. Instead, he entrusted himself to him who judges justly. He himself bore our sins in his body on the tree, so that we might die to sins and live for righteousness; by his wounds you have been healed" (1 Peter 2:22-24).

WHY WAS JESUS WILLING TO SUFFER AND DIE?

Because He loves us and He was obedient to God, His Father.

Jesus said,

"My command is this; Love each other as I have loved you. Greater love has no one than this, that one lay down his life for his friends. ***You are my friends if you do what I command"*** (John 15:12-14).

Jesus also said

". . . the world must learn that I love the Father and that I do exactly what my Father has commanded me" (John 14:31). (See also Romans 5:6-8)

Jesus was in great tribulation knowing He would soon be crucified. Shortly before soldiers came and seized Him, He knelt down and prayed,

"Father, if you are willing, take this cup from me; yet not my will, but yours be done" (Luke 22:42).

"He was oppressed and afflicted, yet he did not open his mouth; he was led like a lamb to slaughter" (Isaiah 53:7).

Jesus obeyed God unto death—cruel death on a cross, and as a result, He overcame the power of sin and death so that we can be saved from eternal punishment. But, we must also obey God unto death, just as Jesus did. (Luke 9:62)

WHY IS THERE A SEPARATION BETWEEN GOD AND US?

We are separated from God because of our sins.

WHAT IS SIN?

Sin is transgression of God's law.

"Everyone who sins breaks the law; in fact, sin is lawlessness" (I John 3:4).

WHO HAS SINNED?

Romans 3:23 says *"for* ***all*** *have sinned and fall short of the glory of God,"*

"We ***all****, like sheep, have gone astray, each of us has turned to his own way; and the Lord has laid on him* [Jesus]

the iniquity of us all" (Isaiah 53:6).

Jesus had the power to send that mocking crowd, and all of us, straight to hell, but He didn't. Instead, out of love and obedience, He shed His blood and died for us.

IS HELL A REAL PLACE?

Yes, the Bible clearly warns us about hell. It tells us that hell is a *"lake of fire"* (Revelation 20:14). Matthew 13:40-42 refers to hell as *"the fiery furnace, where there will be weeping and gnashing of teeth"* and Matthew 25:41 describes hell as *"the eternal fire prepared for the devil and his angles."*

WHO SAVES US FROM OUR SINS, HELL, AND SPIRITUAL DEATH?

Only God can save us. We cannot save ourselves.
"For it is by [God's] *grace that you have been saved, through faith—this is not from yourselves, it is the gift of God—not by works, so that no one can boast. For we are God's workmanship, created in Christ Jesus to do good works, which God prepared in advance for us to do"* (Ephesians 2:8-10).

Romans 6:23 says,
"For the wages of sin is death, but the gift of God is eternal life in Christ Jesus our Lord."

WHO DOES GOD WANT TO BE SAVED?

"God our Savior, wants all men to be saved and come to the knowledge of the truth" (I Timothy 2:3-4 RSV).

"The Lord is not slow in keeping his promise, as some understand slowness. He is patient with you, not wanting anyone to perish, but everyone to come to repentance" (2 Peter 3:9).

DOES THE OLD TESTAMENT HAVE ANY VALUE FOR US TODAY?

Yes, the Old Testament is very good—don't let me mislead you.

But the New Testament tells us what God requires us to do to be forgiven of our sins today. The New Testament also provides us with guidance for living in todays world.

In the Old Testament, God told Noah to build an ark in a land where it had never rained. He told Noah it would save him and his family from the flood He was going to send to the entire earth. God gave Noah specific instructions on how to build the ark and what to take on it.

> *"Noah did everything just as God commanded him"* (Genesis 6:22).

As a result, Noah and his wife and his sons and their wives were saved from destruction (the flood). Noah obeyed God to the exact measure.

In another Old Testament story, God told Abraham,

> *"Take your son, your only son Isaac, whom you love, and go to the region of Moriah. Sacrifice him there as a burnt offering on one of the mountains I will tell you about"* (Genesis 22:2).

Abraham was probably very sad and upset when God requested him to sacrifice Isaac, but he did not argue with God or question Him. Instead, he remained faithful.

> *"Early the next morning Abraham got up and saddled his donkey. He took with him two of his servants and his son Isaac. When he had cut enough wood for the burnt offering, he set out for the place God had told him about"* (Genesis 22:3). *"When they reached the place God had told him about, Abraham built an altar there and arranged the wood on it. He bound his son Isaac and laid him on the altar, on top of the wood. Then he reached out his hand and took the knife to slay his son. But the angel of the Lord called out to him from heaven, 'Abraham! Abraham!' 'Here I am,' he replied. 'Do not lay a hand on the boy,' he said. 'Do not do anything to him.' Now I know that you fear God, because you have not withheld from me your only son'"* (Genesis 22:9-12).

Abraham obeyed the Lord and his son was allowed to live. Both Noah and Abraham demonstrated a tremendous amount of faith when their belief in God, turned to obedience.

As in the days of Noah and Abraham, God also tests our faith today to see if we really love Him. Before we continue, we need to understand what Faith is? We can see even as in the examples above, **Faith is a general term which requires both believing and obeying.** What would have happened to Noah if he would have told God, "I believe you will send a flood, but I don't think it is necessary to build an ark?" (See Hebrews 11:7) Would Noah have been saved? No, it was Noah's faith (belief and obedience) in God and His plan that saved him from perishing. Will believing without obedience save us? James 2:19 says,

> *"You believe that there is one God. Good! Even the demons believe that—and shudder."*

The demons believe, but they are not saved. Why? Because we are saved by faith and faith requires both belief and obedience. If we have one without the other, we have not faith. Let's look at John 3:36 (RSV):

> *"He who believes in the Son has eternal life; he who does not obey the Son shall not see life, but the wrath of God rests upon him."*

Romans 2:13 says:

> *"For it is not those who hear the law who are righteous in God's sight, but it is those who obey the law who will be declared righteous."*

And, Jesus said,

> *"If anyone loves me, he will obey my teaching. He who does not love me will not obey my teaching. These words you hear are not my own; they belong to the Father who sent me"* (John 14:23a-24b).

By the grace of God, we can all be saved—through faith (belief and obedience). God's will strongly implies that our belief in Him must be accompanied by obedience if we are to please Him. Once **we hear the word** and **believe in God**, scripture tells us that we must **repent of our sins**.

WHAT DOES REPENT MEAN?

Repent means to be sorry and turn away from our transgressions (sinful or ungodly ways).

> *"In the past God overlooked such ignorance, but now he commands all people everywhere to repent" Acts 17:30).*

Because Jesus humbled himself unto death for us, God requires us to **confess that Jesus is Lord.**

"That if you confess with your mouth, 'Jesus is Lord,' and believe in your heart that God raised him from the dead, you will be saved" Romans 10:9).

THERE IS ONE MORE COMMANDMENT GOD AND JESUS REQUIRE FOR SALVATION.

Scripture tells us that we must be baptized. Before Jesus ascended into heaven, He left us with vital instructions. His final words . . . words spoken last, so we would remember them most, were . . .

"All authority in heaven and on earth has been given to me. ***Therefore go and make disciples of all nations, baptizing them in the name of the Father and of the Son and of the Holy Spirit, and teaching them to obey everything that I have commanded you.*** *And surely I will be with you always, to the very end of the age" Matthew 28:18-20).*

Mark 16:16 says,

"Whoever believes and is baptized will be saved, *but whoever does not believe will be condemned."*

Someone once told me, "I feel that I am a saved Christian but I have never been baptized." **IS BAPTISM REALLY NECESSARY FOR SALVATION?**

Since Jesus commanded baptism, it should never be an issue of debate. Unfortunately, Bible baptism is one of the most contradicted issues in todays religious society. Because of that, I would like to encourage every person who loves the Lord, or desires to become a Christian, to make it a priority to study baptism and the important role it plays in our salvation.

Before we study its importance, we need to understand what it is.

The Bible speaks about several different baptisms and when I studied them in detail I learned and understood the Bible even more clearly. To study them all would be a whole lesson in itself, so for now, I would like to concentrate on the original baptism and the one Apostle Paul referred to more than twenty years after the church began (in the book of Acts). In Ephesians 4:4-5 Paul wrote, *"There is one Body and one Spirit — just as you were called to one hope when you were called — **one Lord, one faith, one baptism.**"*

The **one baptism** we can still practice today is the original water baptism.

WHAT IS WATER BAPTISM ACCORDING TO SCRIPTURE?

The Bible makes it very clear that God's (water) baptism requires going down into the water (Acts 8:38) and coming up out of the water (Matthew 3:16). There was always "much water". The original Biblical Greek word for baptize is "baptizo", which means to immerse, dip, plunge, emerge, or submerge.

When I looked at immerse, dip, plunge, emerge, and submerge in my common dictionary I learned that those words mean to put something under an enveloping medium, to cover with water, to bury, to arise out of an unfortunate state, to plunge under and to baptize.

There are other Greek words for pour or sprinkle. Those are "cheo" (to pour) and "rantizo" (to sprinkle). Water baptism is an immersion.

WHAT IS THE PURPOSE OF WATER BAPTISM AND WHY IS IT SO IMPORTANT?

In the book of Acts when the Lord's church was first being established, we learn that belief and baptism went hand in hand. Because of its importance, **new converts to Christianity were baptized** (immersed) **immediately upon believing the gospel message**, because **this is when their sins were forgiven.** Once their sins were washed away **they received the gift of the Holy Spirit** — a necessity for eternal life. (Refer to Romans 8:9 for further study.) Let's look now at a few of the biblical accounts provided for us in the book of Acts.

> *"Peter replied, '**Repent and be baptized everyone of you, in the name of Jesus Christ so that your sins may be forgiven. And you will receive the gift of the Holy Spirit**'"* (Acts 2:38).

"Those who accepted the gospel message were baptized, and about three thousand were added to their number that day" (Acts (2:41).

Paul (Saul) was baptized before he began his work for the Lord (Acts 9:18). The Ethiopian eunuch saw the importance of baptism and was baptized along the roadside as soon as he found **much water** (Acts 8:26-39).

The jailer and his family were also baptized immediately upon believing in the Lord Jesus, even though it was the middle of the night (Acts 16:25-34).

As we proceed through scripture we learn even more about the purpose of baptism.

When we study the parable of the wedding banquet in Matthew 22:1-14, we are warned that: 1) the day is coming when God no longer keeps inviting those who refuse Him, and 2) those who do come to Him must come clothed properly and on God's terms or they will be thrown out into outer darkness where there will be weeping and gnashing of teeth.

Galatians 3:26-27 tells us that baptism clothes us with Christ.

"You are all sons of God through faith [belief and obedience] ***in Christ Jesus, for all of you who were baptized into Christ have clothed yourself with Christ."***

The gospel message proclaims the death, burial and resurrection of Jesus.

AS CHRISTIANS, THE BIBLE TELLS US THAT WE ARE TO IMITATE CHRIST JESUS.

In 1 Peter 2:21 we read
"To this you were called, because Christ suffered for you, leaving you an example, that you should follow in his steps."

1 John 2:6 says
"Whoever claims to live in him must walk as Jesus did."

Jesus lived, died on the cross (crucified), was buried, rose from the dead, stayed on earth a little while longer, and then ascended into heaven. We are to live, die to our sins, (crucified with Christ) by being buried in baptism, raise to walk the new life on earth, remain faithful, and someday go to heaven to be with God forever.

The Bible says that baptism is a "burial". When something is buried, it is put under ground. When we are spiritually buried with Christ, we are put under water (immersed).

The Bible asks,
"Or don't you know that all of us who were baptized into Christ Jesus were baptized into his death? ***We were therefore buried with him through baptism into death in order that, just as Christ was raised from the dead through the glory of the Father, we too may live a new life."***

"If we have been united with him in his death, we will certainly also be united with him in his resurrection. For we know that our old self was crucified with him so that the body of sin might be rendered powerless, that we should no longer be slaves to sin—because anyone who has died has been freed from sin."

"Now if we die with Christ, we believe that we will also live with him. For we know that since Christ was raised from the dead, he cannot die again; death no longer has mastery over him. The death he died, he died to sin once for all; but the life he lives, he lives to God. In the same way, count yourselves dead to sin but alive to God in Christ Jesus" (Romans 6:3-11). *"Those who belong to Christ have crucified the sinful nature with its passions and desires"* (Galatians 5:24).

Before Jesus died, Nicodemus was confused.
"'How can a man be born when he is old?' Nicodemus asked. 'Surely he cannot enter a second time into his mother's womb to be born!' Jesus answered, 'I tell you the truth, unless a man is born of water and the Spirit, he cannot enter the kingdom of God. Flesh gives birth to flesh, but the Spirit gives birth to spirit'" (John 3:5-7).
Jesus told this already religious man, that we must be born again.

Baptism gives us new birth. 1 Peter 1:22-23 says,
*"****Now that you have purified yourselves by obeying the truth*** *so that you have sincere love for your brothers, love one another deeply, from the heart.* ***For you have been born again,*** *not of*

perishable seed, but of imperishable, through the living and enduring word of God."

Long ago, when God waited patiently in the days of Noah, while the ark was being built, men continued to sin.

"In it [the ark] *only a few people, eight in all, were saved through water.* ***This water symbolizes baptism that now saves you also****—not in the removal of dirt from the body but the pledge of a good conscience toward God"* (1 Peter 3:20b-21).

From the biblical references discussed above, we have obtained valuable information. We can easily conclude that water baptism was commanded by Jesus, His spirit filled apostles taught water baptism by immersion and new converts to Christianity were baptized immediately upon believing. We also discovered that the first century Christian did not even consider salvation without water baptism because of its importance.

We also learned from scripture that baptism clothes us with Christ. Water baptism is a burial, as well as, a new birth (new life). This simple act of **obedience** also gives us the privilege of a **clear conscious towards God, forgiveness of sins and, Gods precious gift of the Holy Spirit.** There is nothing special about the water but there are many special things about God's grace and the miracle He performs in us when we obey Him.

IF GOD'S BAPTISM REQUIRES MUCH WATER, THEN WHY WAS TOM SPRINKLED AS AN INFANT? WHERE DID INFANT SPRINKLING COME FROM?

Infant sprinkling was introduced and accepted by men, basically for convenience, several hundred years after the death and resurrection of Jesus Christ. Jesus did not teach or command it. He himself (our divine example) demonstrated the way, and was baptized by immersion in the Jordan River. He was perfect, so it was not because He was a sinner, but the Bible says it was to

"fulfill all righteousness." ***"As soon as Jesus was baptized, he went up out of the water. At that moment heaven was opened, and he saw the Spirit of God descending like a dove and lighting on Him. And a voice from heaven said, 'This is my Son whom I love; with him I am well pleased'"*** (Matthew 3:15b-16).

WILL SMALL CHILDREN GO TO HELL IF THEY DIE, BUT ARE NOT SPRINKLED?

Like all other questions, let me answer this based on biblical facts. God is the "Only and Final Judge," and His judgment is just. We are saved by "faith" (belief and obedience). *"Consequently, faith comes from hearing the message, and the message is heard through the word of Christ"* (Romans 10:17). In each biblical account, people who wanted salvation were:

1) old enough to understand what sin is and who God is,
2) old enough to repent of their sins and confess Jesus as Lord,
3) old enough to willingly obey God and His instructions for salvation and live a new life in Christ.

Innocent little babies and small children are not capable of doing these things. When children start feeling guilty for their mistakes, they become accountable and must choose which direction they want for their lives. Christianity is a choice. Romans 14:12 tells us that *"each of us will give an account of himself to God."* Jesus said,

> *"Let the little children come to me, and do not hinder them, for the kingdom of God belongs to such as these"* (Mark 10:14).

As a matter of fact, He even wants adults to become like children; receiving Him with humble loving trust.

> *"I tell you the truth, anyone who will not receive the kingdom of God like a little child will never enter it"* (Mark 10:15).

IS "SPRINKLING" MENTIONED ANYWHERE IN THE BIBLE?

Yes, it is. The Old Testament teaches us about sprinkling not only for sin offerings, but for other spiritual offerings as well (see Leviticus for examples). There was one vital difference however—animal blood was always used, not water. *"In fact, the law requires that nearly everything be cleansed with blood, and without the shedding of blood, there is no forgiveness of sins"* (Hebrews 9:22). New Testament scriptures always refer to Christ's blood (see 1 Peter 1:2) since His blood replaced all animal sacrifices from the Old

Testament. Hebrews 10:22 says,

"Having our hearts sprinkled to cleanse us from a guilty conscience and having our bodies washed with pure water."

When we submit to baptism and are immersed into Christ, we contact the blood of Christ. Our bodies are washed with pure water and the Lord cleanses our hearts.

WHY IS THERE SO MUCH CONFLICT BETWEEN RELIGIOUS GROUPS OVER GOD'S WORD, (THE HOLY BIBLE) AND WHY DO PEOPLE BELIEVE IN SO MANY DIFFERENT WAYS OF SALVATION?
HAVE GOD'S ORIGINAL TEACHINGS FOR SALVATION CHANGED OVER THE YEARS?

No, God's teachings for salvation have not changed over the years.

Unfortunately, even in the time period shortly after Christ died, there was quarreling amongst the Christians. *"One of you says, 'I follow Paul;' another, 'I follow Apollos;' another, 'I follow Cephas;' still another, 'I follow Christ.' Is Christ divided?"* (1 Corinthians 1:12b-13a)

In Galatians 1:6-10, the apostle Paul, sent not by men but by God, was upset with false teachers who were coming in and upsetting his work of truth.

We must realize that Jesus built **one** church, and **one** church only. Men have built **many** churches. The bible tells us in Acts 5:29 that,

"We must obey God—rather than men!"

Hebrews 12:2 says,
"Let us fix our eyes on Jesus, the author and perfecter of the faith . . ."

The Bible also warns us in Timothy 4:3-4,
"For the time will come when men will not put up with sound doctrine. Instead, to suit their own desires, they will gather around them a great number of teachers to say what their itching ears want to hear. They will turn their ears away from the truth and turn aside to myths."

This is happening now. Please don't get caught in the devil's trap! Twisted scriptures, cults, and counterfeit teachings surround us and, sadly, look so authentic. Many people feel saved, but unfortunately, feelings can be deceiving. The Bible says, Satan is the father of lies (see John 8:42-47). A lie is a falsehood. God's plan for salvation is so beautiful and simple. Satan doesn't care how sincere or how spiritual we are. All he is concerned about is keeping us from being clothed with the blood of Christ, because if he succeeds at that, we still belong to him!

2 Corinthians 11:14b-15a warns us that
"Satan himself masquerades as an angel of light. It is not surprising then, if his servants masquerade as servants of righteousness."

"Dear friends, do not believe every spirit, but test the spirits to see whether they are from God, because many false prophets have gone out into the World" (1 John 4:1).

(For further study, see also Matthew 7:21-23 and Galations 1:6-9.)

Jesus said,
"Blessed are those who wash their robes, that they may have the right to the tree of life and may go through the gates into the city. Outside are the dogs, those who practice magic arts, the sexually immoral, the murderers, the idolaters and everyone who loves and practices falsehood" (Revelation 22:14-15).

It is important for us to remember that God is God. The Lord is not impressed with man's opinion and He is angered by false teachings.

"There is a way that seems right to a man, but in the end it leads to [spiritual] *death"* (Proverbs 14:12).

John the Baptist prepared **the way** (Matthew 3:1-6). Jesus demonstrated **the way** (Matthew 3:16-17). And Jesus said, *"I am the way and the truth and the life. No one comes to the Father except through me"* (John 14:6).

Many people sincerely love the Lord, but are sincerely misled. Paul (Saul) was, but when he learned the truth, he obeyed. The whole purpose of this life is to obey and serve the Lord. He did so much for us. As believers in Christ, we need to be united as well. Satan loves nothing more than spiritual weakness and division. The word Christian bears great responsibilities and those who claim it, need to adhere closely to the doctrines of our precious Lord and Saviour, Jesus Christ. The desire and goal of every Christian should be to imitate Christ and then stand firm, in all circumstances, with unwavering faith, for what is right and true.

God loves each one of us, but He will never force us to love and obey Him. He has given us a free will. If we refuse to completely obey the teachings that God created and Jesus taught, then we are saying "no" to God and "yes" to Satan and hell. I am sharing this not to upset or confuse you, but because I love you and care about your soul. These things are not based on my opinions nor man's rules, but rather on the unchanging Word of God.

Once we learn God's truth, the Lord wants us to:

"Do everything without complaining or arguing so that you many become blameless and pure, children of God without fault in a crooked and depraved generation" (Philippians 2:14-15a).

"Repent and be baptized, every one of you, in the name of Jesus Christ so that your sins may be forgiven. And you will receive the gift of the Holy Spirit" (Acts 2:38).

DO YOU NEED TO SET A DATE WHEN YOU WANT TO BE SAVED?

No.

"I tell you, now is the time of God's favor, now is the day of salvation" (2 Corinthians 6:2b).

Please don't wait. It's too risky to hold out until we get that new home or car, our own business, our next college degree, or whatever else it is that holds us back from obeying God. James 4:14 says,

"Why you do not even know what will happen tomorrow. What is your life? You are a mist that appears for a little while and then vanishes."

I urge you, be very careful. Nothing is as important as eternal life. Once we die, it is too late. Jesus is coming back to take His people home to live with Him for eternity. Will you be ready to meet Him when He calls your name?

> *"'Come now, let us reason together,' says the Lord. 'Though your sins are like scarlet, they shall be as white as snow; though they are red as crimson, they shall be like wool. If you are willing and obedient, you will eat the best from the land; but if you resist and rebel, you will be devoured by the sword.' For the mouth of the Lord has spoken"* (Isaiah 1:18-20).

When we obey God's plan of salvation, including baptism by immersion, we are not doing anything to earn our salvation. We are simply accepting the Lord, His love, His grace, His forgiveness and His special gift to us, the Holy Spirit. We are saved because **God** is good—not because **we** are good. Belief and obedience mark only the beginning of our walk with Christ. Christianity is a life long commitment. The old must pass and we must remain faithful and obedient to God and His ways all the days of our lives. (See Revelation 2:10) Christianity also means that we are heirs of a wonderful God. It means salvation, eternal life, happiness and joy.

Our lives are like seasons. Don't miss out on the real **"Beauty of Spring"** and the hope of eternal life in heaven with our Lord.

> *"The Lord is compassionate and gracious,*
> *slow to anger, abounding in love.*
> *He will not always accuse, nor will he harbor his anger forever;*
> *he does not treat us as our sins deserve or repay us according to our iniquities.*
> *For as high as the heavens are above the earth,*
> *so great is his love for those who fear him;*
> *as far as the east is from the west, so far has he removed our transgressions from us.*
> *As a father has compassion on his children,*
> *so the Lord has compassion on those who fear him;*
> *for he knows how we are formed, he remembers that we are dust.*
> *As for man, his days are like grass,*

he flourishes like a flower of the field;
the wind blows over it and it is gone,
and its place remembers it no more.
But from everlasting to everlasting the Lord's love is with those who fear him, and his righteousness with their children's children — with those who keep his covenant and remember to obey his precepts.
The Lord has established his throne in heaven, and his kingdom rules over all.
Praise the Lord, you His angels, you mighty ones who do his bidding, who obey His word.
Praise the Lord, all His heavenly hosts, you his servants who do his will.
Praise the Lord, all his works are everywhere in his dominion. Praise the Lord, O my soul!"

(Psalm 103:8-22)

Thank you Lord for saving my soul. On this ______ day of ________________________, _______, after hearing the Word of God, believing, repenting of my sins, and confessing Jesus as Lord, I was baptized (immersed) for the forgiveness of my sins and I received the promised gift of the Holy Spirit.

I now promise God that I will remain faithful unto death, regardless of the trials ahead, so that I can live with Him for eternity.

____

Your Signature

God bless you and best wishes in your **"New Life"** with Christ.

1) Do you have specific questions concerning this lesson on eternal salvation?

2) Are you interested in Bible correspondence lessons?

3) Do you desire information on the location of a New Testament Church in your area?

4) Would you be interested in receiving a monthly newsletter from The Beauty of Spring Christian Ministries?

5) Has this book been helpful to you in any way?

If you answered yes to any of the above questions, we would love to hear from you.

Please enclose a business size #10 self addressed stamped envelope and write to:

The Beauty of Spring Christian Ministries
9121 East Tanque Verde Rd., Suite 105-222
Tucson, AZ 85749

P.S. If you are led by God to help financially, in supporting this ministry, please send donations made out to the Beauty of Spring Christian Ministries to the above address. All proceeds will go towards reaching out for Christ. Thank you for supporting His work,

Debbie Schmid

YES! I have enjoyed or benefited from reading this book and I am excited to share it with my friends or family members.

You may order this book by sending $7.00 per copy plus $2.50 shipping and handling to:

The Beauty of Spring
Christian Ministries
9121 E. Tanque Verde Rd., Suite 105-222
Tucson, AZ 85749

or

Joy Publishing
P.O. Box 827
San Juan Capistrano, CA 92675